THE ART

OF

Manufacturing Soap and Candles.

VALUABLE BOOKS

FOR

DRUGGISTS, CHEMISTS, &c.

PIESSE ON THE ART OF PERFUMERY, and the Methods of Obtaining the Odors of Plants, with Instructions for the Manufacture of Perfumes for the Handkerchief, Scented Powders, Odorous Vinegars, Dentifrices, Pomatums, Cosmetics, Perfumed Soap, &c.; to which is added an Appendix on Preparing Artificial Fruit Essences, &c. By G. W. SEPTIMUS PIESSE, Analytical Chemist, Author of "Chemical, Natural, and Physical Magic," "The Laboratory of Chemical Wonders," &c. Second American from the Third London Edition. Price, $3 00

COOLEY'S TOILET AND COSMETIC ARTS. The Toilet and Cosmetic Arts, in Ancient and Modern Times. With a Review of the Different Theories of Beauty and copious allied Information, Social, Hygienic, and Medical, including Instructions and Cautions respecting the selection and use of Perfumes, Cosmetics, and other Toilet Articles; and a *Comprehensive Collection of Formulæ*, and Directions for their Preparation. By ARNOLD J. COOLEY, Author of "Cyclopædia of Receipts, Processes, Data, and Collateral Information, &c., in the Arts and Manufactures." One Volume, thick Demy Octavo. Price, $5 00

MORFIT'S CHEMICAL AND PHARMACEUTICAL MANIPULATIONS. A Manual of the Mechanical and Chemico-Mechanical Operations of the Laboratory, for the use of Chemists, Druggists, Manufacturers, &c. A Second and much enlarged Edition. By CAMPBELL MORFIT, Professor of Analytic and Applied Chemistry in the University of Maryland; assisted by CLARENCE MORFIT, Assistant Melter and Refiner in the United States Assay Office. With 500 Illustrations. Octavo, Leather. Price, $5 00

WETHERILL ON THE MANUFACTURE OF VINEGAR, Theoretical and Practical, with especial Reference to the Quick Process. With Rules for Testing its Purity, &c. &c., and Illustrations. By CHARLES M. WETHERILL, M.D. Price, $1 50

BRANSTON'S HANDBOOK OF PRACTICAL RECEIPTS OF EVERYDAY USE. A Manual for the Chemist, Druggist, Manufacturer, &c. By THOMAS F. BRANSTON. Price, $1 50

BEASLEY'S DRUGGISTS' GENERAL RECEIPT BOOK. Fifth American Edition. Price, $3 50

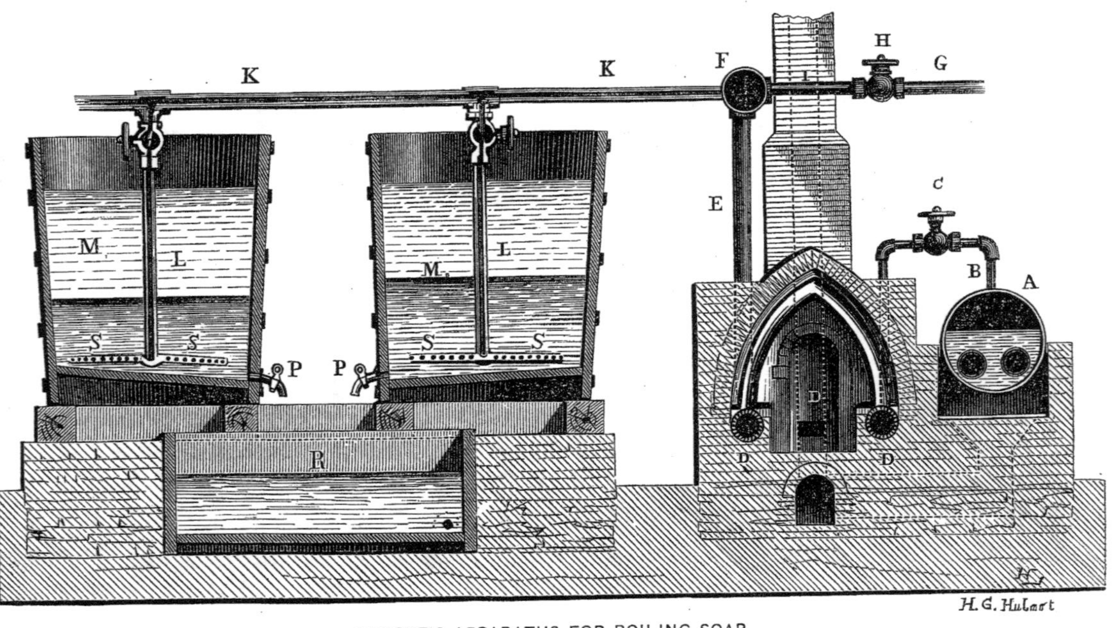

HUBERT'S APPARATUS FOR BOILING SOAP.

THE

ART OF MANUFACTURING

SOAP AND CANDLES,

INCLUDING THE MOST RECENT DISCOVERIES,

EMBRACING

ALL KINDS OF ORDINARY HARD, SOFT, AND TOILET SOAPS, ESPECIALLY THOSE MADE BY THE COLD PROCESS,

THE MODES OF DETECTING FRAUDS,

AND THE MAKING OF

TALLOW AND COMPOSITE CANDLES.

BY ADOLPH OTT, PH.D.,
PRACTICAL AND ANALYTICAL CHEMIST.

PHILADELPHIA:
LINDSAY & BLAKISTON.
1867.

SHERMAN & CO., PRINTERS.

TO

P. H. VAN DER WEYDE, M.D.,

LATE PROFESSOR OF THE NATURAL SCIENCES AND HIGHER MATHEMATICS IN THE COOPER UNION; OF CHEMISTRY AND TOXICOLOGY AT THE NEW YORK MEDICAL COLLEGE; AND OF THE INDUSTRIAL SCIENCES IN THE GIRARD COLLEGE, PHILADELPHIA,

THIS WORK

IS DEDICATED,

WITH THE ESTEEM AND SINCERE REGARD OF

THE AUTHOR.

PREFACE.

In preparing this work, it was not my intention to publish a mere collection of the rich and scattered materials, which literature has furnished on the subject treated (however acceptable it might have been in itself), but to give a clear and concise account of the art of soap and candle making as is now practised. And as my principal design has been to render this volume practical in its character, I have not confined my remarks simply to the manufacture of these articles, but added appropriate illustrations and critical explanations of the various manipulations and mechanical arrangements by which they are effected, thus compiling, instead of a dry compendium of facts, a condensed narrative, both instructive and interesting to the reader, in which are, moreover, introduced matter never previously published.

In the execution of my task, I have derived occasional advantage by the perusal, and made abbreviated quotations from the writings of able and established authors.

With the exception of a few cuts relating to the manufacture of candles, borrowed from "Bolley's Beleuchtungswesen," Part I, all the cuts are original, and prepared by the skilful and artistic draughtsman, Mr. Hubert, of New York.

For a more comprehensive collection of formulæ for perfuming soaps, I must refer the reader to Piesse on the "Art and Manufacture of Perfumery," a work recently issued by Messrs. Lindsay & Blakiston, of Philadelphia.

ADOLPH OTT.

NEW YORK, May 1, 1867.

CONTENTS.

PART I.

ON THE MANUFACTURE OF SOAP.

APPARATUS AND RAW MATERIALS.

CHAPTER I.

CHAPTER II.

CHAPTER III.

CHAPTER IV.

CHAPTER V.

PART II.

ON THE MANUFACTURE OF SOAP.

CHAPTER I.

CHAPTER II.

CHAPTER III.

CHAPTER IV.

CHAPTER V.

PART III.

ON THE MANUFACTURE OF CANDLES.

ERRATA.

On page 35, for "Morfit's Steam Jacket." read "Morfit's Steam Twirl."
" 59, fifth line from top, for "0.9 of 0," read "0.970."
" 67, tenth line from top, for "made fed," read "mast-fed."
" 96, third line from bottom, for "the method of preparing them requires large percentages," &c., read "large percentages of soluble glass were introduced in them," &c.

SOAP MANUFACTURE.

HISTORICAL.

The art of manufacturing soap has been, in a measure, known and followed for many ages, proving a source of industry and advantage to various nations and individuals. It may therefore interest some of our readers if we attempt to trace its origin and progress as indicated by the writings of the earlier authors. Pliny, for instance, the Roman historian, informs us that the art of manufacturing soap is the invention of the Gauls, and that the best article made by them was a combination of goats' tallow and the ashes of the beech-tree. They also seem to have been acquainted with both hard and soft soaps. The Romans eventually acquired this knowledge from the Gauls, by whom this branch of industry was, with their conquests, soon spread over Europe.

Whoever may have been the originators of soapmaking, the Romans were undoubtedly familiar with it. Galen, at least, mentions it in his works, and confirmatory of this statement, we may add that a soapmaker's shop, with its utensils and products, was discovered among the ruins and ashes of Pompeii, which was destroyed by an eruption of Mount Vesuvius in the first century of the Christian era. Soap was often used by the Romans as a cosmetic, for

Pliny tells us that soap, with which the Germans colored their hair red, was imported into Rome for the use of the fashionable ladies and their gallants in that city. This cosmetic was probably tinged with the juice of a plant. But before we recur further to less remote times, we will endeavor to answer the question, "What substitutes were employed previous to the invention of soap?"

Soap, both hard and soft, as it is well known, is produced by the union of the fats and the alkalies; by hard soap, we mean such as have soda, and by soft soap is understood that which has potassa for its basis. Water alone will not remove oily substances from any surfaces to which they may adhere, but a solution of soap, being always more or less alkaline, though its constituents may be united in their number of equivalents, will, nevertheless, render the oil freely miscible with water, so that it can be easily erased. A similar effect is produced by using a mixture of water and lixivious salts. The gall of animals and the juice of certain plants, also possess the property of removing dust and dirt. It does not, however, appear that gall was employed by the ancients, but it is certain that in washing they used saponaceous plants. In the remotest times, it appears that clothes were cleaned by being rubbed or stamped upon in water without the addition of any substance whatever. We are told by Homer, that Nausicaa and her attendants, washed their garments by treading upon them in pits containing water. We find, however, at a later period, that mention is made of ashes and a lye of ashes, but it is so seldom noticed that their primary use cannot be ascertained. Aristophanes and Plato mention a substance, "*konia*," which they say was employed for washing purposes, and Pollax leads us to infer that this "*konia*" was a lye of ashes. With this lye, oil and wine jars were cleansed, as well as the images of the gods. The practice of decarbonizing alkaline lyes by means of lime, was, according to Beckmann, known at any rate in the time of Paulus Ægineta, but we are not led to suppose that the Romans were acquainted with the dry substance obtained by evaporation of the clear liquid.

Various ancient writers inform us, furthermore, that lixivious natural salts were employed for washing, such as the *nitrum*, designated "*borith*" in the writings of the Hebrews. In the present day it has commonly been supposed equivalent to *nitre*, but this is an error, for it has been evidently proved that the ancients understood by the word *nitrum*, the carbonated alkali either of potassa or soda. Both of these substances are natural products, and found in many places and in large quantities, either in outcrops of different rocks or prairies, or in springs and lakes. Asia is rich in such lakes; some exist in Asia Minor, Armenia, Persia, Hindostan, Thibet, and other eastern parts of that continent. Egypt, also, is richly supplied with soda lakes and springs, and with mineral sodas, whilst in Naples a volcano rock is still extant containing soda. As some of these substances are highly impregnated with hygroscopic salts, it is not necessary to suppose, as some do, that the Egyptians produced their mineral alkali from the ashes of plants; on the contrary, Pliny states that they were obliged to put it in well-corked vessels, otherwise it would become liquid. The production of alkali from plants seems to have been the invention of a later period.

Strabo speaks of an alkaline water in Armenia, which we have reason to believe is similar to that of the lake Ascanius mentioned by Aristotle, Anxigonus Carystrius, and Pliny. And here it is worthy of remark, that the ancients made ointments of those mineral alkalies and oil, but no hard soap.

The cheapest and most common article, however, used for washing was the urine of men and animals. This, not long since, was actually employed in the cloth manufactories at Leeds, Halifax, and other places in England. To obtain a supply of it, the ancients deposited at the corners of the streets, special vessels, which they emptied as soon as filled by the passers-by, who were at liberty, even expected, to use them. Scourers at Rome, however, were obliged to reside either in the suburbs or in unfrequented streets, on account of the consequent disagreeable odor attending their business.

Instead of soap, the ancients at any rate made use of the saponaceous juice of some plant, but of which one it is difficult, we may say impossible, to define. Pliny speaks, among others, of a plant growing on a rocky soil and on the mountains, with prickly and rough leaves. Fuchs was of the opinion that it must have been the *soap-wort*, still used in Italy and France. Others imagine that it was the *Gypsophila Struthium*, of Linné, a plant with a tender stem and leaves like those of the olive tree; but Beckmann places no confidence in any of these surmises, but rather favors the idea that it was a plant growing in Syria. Bean-meal was also employed for cleansing purposes.

Large quantities of fullers' earth (silicate of alumina), at the same time were moreover used, and clothes, dressed with this earth, were stamped upon by the feet, a process by which grease is partly absorbed and partly scoured off. The poor at Rome, moreover, rubbed it over their clothes at festivals, in order that they might appear brighter. Some of these earths were employed in the baths instead of *nitrum*, and De la Valle, who travelled through the Levant at the beginning of the last century, states that the practice was still in vogue and adopted by persons of the highest distinction; they, in fact, never bathing without it.

It has, furthermore, been authentically established, that in the eighth century there were numerous soap factories in Italy and Spain, but it was not till the close of the twelfth and commencement of the thirteenth century that this branch of business was gradually introduced into France. The first factories were founded in Marseilles, an old colony of the Phœnicians, a race half Grecian, half Egyptian, energetic, intelligent, active, particularly partial to industrial arts and commercial enterprises. This ancient city was, as it were, the cradle of soap manufacturing. Here all the crude materials for this purpose were abundant. The fecundity of its soil gave rise to the olive tree of the Orient, as well as to the vegetable sodas, whilst its harbor in the Mediterranean peculiarly favored and hastened the prosperity of the soap manufacturers and traders.

There has, indeed, been gradually a considerable increase in the demand for soap, attributable mainly to the method of bleaching linen, first adopted in the seventeenth century, at which time this new branch of manufacture was imported from the West Indies, and the important application of the chlorine for bleaching textile fabrics had not been discovered. Notwithstanding the richness of its soil, and its natural resources, Marseilles, nevertheless, could not furnish the crude materials in quantities sufficient to supply the wants of her soap manufacturers, and consequently, ere long, became tributary to Spain and Italy,—to the former for the oils and vegetable sodas; to the latter for the oils only.

From France, the art of manufacturing soap was introduced into England at an unknown epoch prior to the year 1500. Soap, for a long time, was there made partly according to the French method, viz., with sodas obtained from the incineration of seashore plants, and partly after the German plan with potash and salt, which plan is still followed by some old-fashioned soapmakers. Almost all kinds of soap were thus manufactured in England, whilst in France the olive oil soap only was produced. About the first decennium of the present century, however, palm oil and cocoa oil soaps have been made in Paris, where also the art of manufacturing toilet soaps has scarcely been superseded by either English or American manufacturers. The application of rosin for making soap is of English origin. When the art of soapmaking was introduced into this country, it is difficult to ascertain, but it is certain that the great impulse which the art received originated in 1804, from the genius of Le Blanc, by whom soda was economically extracted from common salt, and eventually introduced into the English market by Mr. James

Muspratt, the owner of extensive chemical works. This discovery, moreover, one of the most beautiful and important in modern chemistry, inaugurated a new era, as it were, in the art of soapmaking. Not less important were the investigations of Chevreul in 1811, by whom the proximate constituents of the fats, scarcely known before, were exactly demonstrated. He, in fact, may justly be regarded as the savant who elevated this industrial branch from a mere trade to a prominent art, which at the present day is characterized by the introduction of new saponifiable substances from all parts of the world, by the application of ordinary and superheated steam, and by various mechanical arrangements for different processes of pressure; quite recently also, use of pressure has been made by which equally mild and detersive soaps are produced at a cheaper rate and less waste of time.

COMPOSITION OF SOAPS.

Soaps are not, as is generally supposed, the result of the direct and integral union of fats with alkalies. The chemical action which produces saponification is of a very complex nature. The art of making soap dates from a very early period, and though it was known that certain fats heated with caustic lyes formed soap, still the theory of the union of oils and alkalies was not satisfactorily ascertained and established till the French chemist, Chevreul, about fifty years ago, unerringly proved—

1st. That all fatty matters known as oils, butters, and suets (with very few exceptions), consisted partly of liquid and partly of solid ingredients, such as the stearine, the margarine, the oleine, the butyrine, &c., &c.

2d. That these ingredients, or proximate principles, are decomposed, by the action of alkalies, into their components, consisting of the sweet principle of fat known as glycerine, and certain fatty acids, called the stearic, margaric, oleic, acids, &c.

3d. That the solidity of mutton suet, of beef tallow, and hog's fat, is chiefly attributable to the stearine and margarine; and the liquidity of oils, to the oleine. Upon this theory, it follows that when fats or oils are heated with caustic lyes, a combination of fatty acids with alkali is formed; this operation is designated saponification. Several attempts have recently been made to substitute petroleum for fatty matters in the manufacture of soap, but had the theory of saponification been fully understood by such parties, they would not have wasted their time and money in so hopeless an enterprise.

Soaps are divided into hard and soft, the former having soda, and the latter potash for their bases. The former, however, is the most extensively manufactured, being universally in demand, whilst that for the latter is very limited, particularly in this country. Acids decompose soaps, combining with their base and expelling the fatty acids, for these latter being insoluble in the former, float on the surface of the liquid. By this means, consequently, soaps are easily analyzed, but on this subject a special chapter is devoted in the present work.

We have deemed it expedient thus briefly to introduce to the notice of the reader, the theory and principles on which saponification is based, for though practice alone can teach one how to make good soap, it is obviously expedient that he should be somewhat acquainted with the laws of chemical affinity, by means of which, those numerous phenomena occurring in the manufacture of soap may be more readily understood.

PART I.

APPARATUS AND RAW MATERIALS.

APPARATUS AND RAW MATERIALS.

CHAPTER I.

APPARATUS REQUIRED FOR BOILING SOAPS, AND THE VARIOUS METHODS FOR HEATING.

Of the Construction and Capacity of the Caldrons.

Whether steam be employed or not, these are made of wood, or wrought-iron, or cast-iron, or bricks lined with glazed stone. Their dimensions necessarily vary from two hundred to four thousand gallons, according to the extent of the manufacture; but the larger the caldron, the better, as much labor, fuel, and lye are thus saved. One hundred pounds of fat will require a thirty-five gallon caldron, and a ton of the same material will need a vessel of a capacity of about seven hundred gallons. The shape is invariably cylindrical, being widest at the top, having usually (indeed they ought always to have) a faucet for the purpose of discharging the spent lye.

Brick Kettles,

though costly, are best in one respect, viz., they retain heat the longest during the paste operation. The bottom of these, if desired, can be composed of brick when steam is employed, whilst in other cases, a metallic bottom is absolutely necessary. As, however, cracks at the juncture are occasionally caused by the unequal expansion of brick and metal, much caution should be exercised in the structure of such kettles. The thickness of the walls also, should be regulated by the size, and the inside built with glazed stone, whilst the whole, exterior and interior, should be cemented with pozzuolan earth mixed with sand. To make them still safer, it would be judicious to hoop them with strong iron clamps.

Fig. 1.

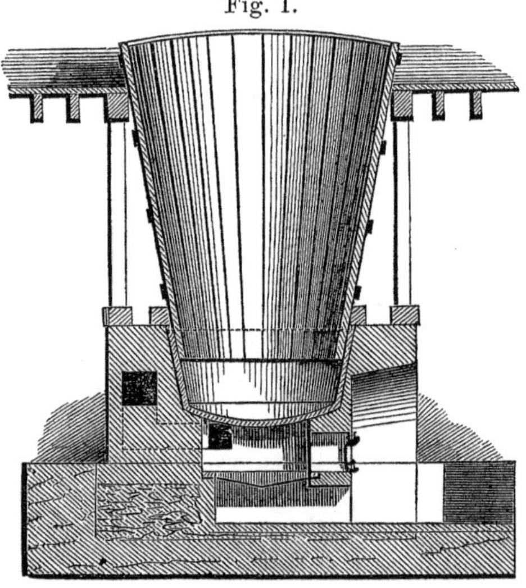

Boiling Pan with a wooden Curb.

The above wood-cut exhibits a boiling-pan with its upper portion constructed of wood. It forms a hollow cone of iron-bound staves, and is fixed water-tight into the rim of the boiler. This is called a curb. It can be made of any size, and is very convenient, inasmuch as it affords ample space for the soap-paste to ascend.

If steam be employed, the *superheated* is preferable, for it can be introduced directly into the material, thereby expediting the heating process, as well as causing a more forcible agitation of the ingredients than the mere crutch by manual exertion can accomplish.

Cast-Iron Kettles

are, for the most part, only found in small factories, for in larger establishments, merely the lower portion is made of cast-iron, and the upper of wood or brick. In purchasing kettles manufactured entirely of cast-iron, the thinnest should be selected, which are always composed of finer and denser grain, and can be more easily filed than the thicker. In every instance, too, the soft iron is preferable to the brittle, being more durable; but with regard to durability, it should be borne in mind that

Sheet-Iron Kettles

will last longer than the cast-iron. They, also, when burnt through, can be satisfactorily repaired, whereas the others are altogether useless, and new ones have to be supplied. Here, again, the *soft* sheet-iron (and that of the first quality) should be selected, the bottom piece being from three-eighths to one-half an inch in thickness, and the sides from three-sixteenths to one-fourth, according to the dimensions. Much attention should also be paid to *rivetting* the pieces so that no aperture be left. The rivets in the lower third, moreover, should be inserted *evenly* with the bottom (countersunk), otherwise the workman cannot go smoothly and thoroughly over it with his crutch,—a necessary process to prevent the soap from burning.

In conclusion, we would observe, that a soft sheet-iron boiler, judiciously heated, and carefully cleaned after each operation, will last five or six years, perhaps longer, without requiring any repairs.

Heating the Pans with Open Fire.

Common kettles, which are to be heated with open fire, should be so constructed that the heat may circulate at the bottom before it enters the chimney. In kettles, however, designed for soap-boiling, the heat must be confined to the bottom, for if it be allowed to circulate around the sides, the ingredients would inevitably be burnt. In order thus to circumscribe and condense the heat, it is necessary that

1st. The grate be placed in the centre of the hearth and vertically below the kettle.

2d. The inside of the fireplace be built of refractory bricks, in order that the heat may be thrown back below the bottom of the kettle.

3d. The fuel employed be that which produces the most heat and the least flame. Hence hard coal should be selected.

4th. The openings through which the products of combustion enter the chimney, possess together the same surface as the grate; experience having shown that this is the best method for obtaining a good draft and effecting a complete combustion of the fuel.

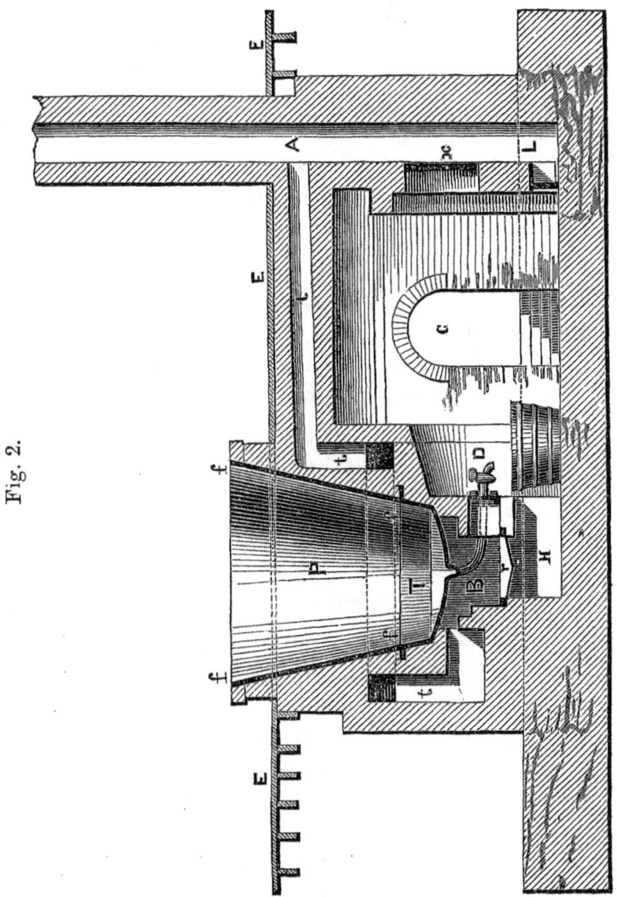

Fig. 2.

The annexed diagram represents a furnace heated by an open fire.

The sides are composed of brickwork, erected and

lined with cement (mortar resisting the action of water). The upper part, *f*, *f*, *f*, *f*, which never comes in contact with the fire, and is intended to afford space for the soap to rise, expands in the form of a cone. The fireplace B is separated from the ash-pit H by the grate *r*. The fire, after having heated the bottom of the pan, passes by the flue *t*, *t*, *t*, half round the side of the pan into the chimney A. This is accessible for the purpose of cleaning by the door X; the soot is thrown into the pit L. A tube, with a cock, leads from the lowest part of the pan for the removal of the under lye. The whole of the pan is sunk into the floor of the boiling-house, which is made of planks, stone, or iron-plate, in such a manner that the brickwork of the upper part projects to about three feet above the floor.

The pans or boilers are calculated to contain 240 cwts. of soap.

Heating Pans with Steam.

Both ordinary and superheated steam (*i. e.*, of a temperature over 212°), are employed for the above purpose; but the latter is far preferable, because, as before stated, the heat can then be introduced directly into the material, whereas ordinary steam has to be condensed through a worm, or conveyed intermediately under a kettle with a double bottom, and a tube for the discharge of the condensed vapor. A worm or such a kettle is requisite, otherwise the quantity of water condensed would be so voluminous, that hard and grain soaps could not be boiled to "strength." By applying superheated steam, now almost universally adopted in chemical establishments, both time and fuel are saved, because such high-pressure steam mingling with the fat, increases the necessary agitation of all the ingredients, thus facilitating and expediting saponification. These advantages not only accrue in large factories, but also in those where they boil perhaps merely twice per week. A steam-boiler, eight feet in length and three feet in diameter, with two atmospheres pressure, will easily manufacture weekly, 100 cwt. of soap.

Again, it should be remembered that much less fuel is consumed in generating steam to obtain a given amount of heat, than when it has to be produced by an open fire; in the former process, also, less watching is requisite, and several vessels can be boiled at the same time, though only one fireplace be used, whilst in the latter much heat is lost by the absorbing effect of the brickwork, and by its unavoidable escape through the chimney.

Among other advantages of steam, we may mention that not only can wooden vessels be used, but also that the temperature can be regulated and kept at a certain degree by simply turning the stop-cocks; the fats combine more readily and rapidly with the alkalies; the boiling is uniform throughout the whole mass, and the soap never burns. The manufacture may be carried on in a smaller building, and the vessels placed on any spot within the range of the steam-generator.

H. G. Hubert's Apparatus for Boiling Soap.

(*See Frontispiece.*)

A is a steam-boiler of ordinary construction; B is a steam-pipe provided with a stop-cock C; D is a steam superheater; E is a pipe leading from the superheater D to the receiver F; G is a pipe supplying air from a force-pump; H is a valve for regulating the introduction of air in the apparatus through the pipe I; F is a receiver where the steam and air are mixed together; K is a pipe conveying the mixed air and steam to any number of soap-boiling apparatus; L L are pipes conveying the steam and air to the bottom of the vats M M′; *s*, *s*, *s*, *s*, are radiating pipes perforated with holes, turned in opposite directions, so that when the air and steam issues from them, they will cause a rotating motion of the whole mass of supernatant liquid in the vats M M′.

R is the tank for receiving the lye drained by the cocks P P′.

The operation of the apparatus is easily understood. The lye and fat being introduced in the vats M M′, steam is allowed to escape gradually in the apparatus D, where it becomes superheated, and is carried over and injected through the mass in the tanks M M′. When it is required that the mass be stirred, then air is introduced in the apparatus by turning the valve H. It will be observed that the workman has a perfect control of the operations, being able by simply turning the cock C or H to increase or diminish the heat and to stir or leave the pasty contents of the vats M M′ at rest.

H. G. Hubert, the inventor of this apparatus, has kindly volunteered the use of his drawings for insertion in this work, and further information can be obtained by addressing him, No. 309 Broadway, New York.

MORFIT'S STEAM JACKET

accomplishes the mixing and boiling of the soap ingredients simultaneously.

Fig. 3.

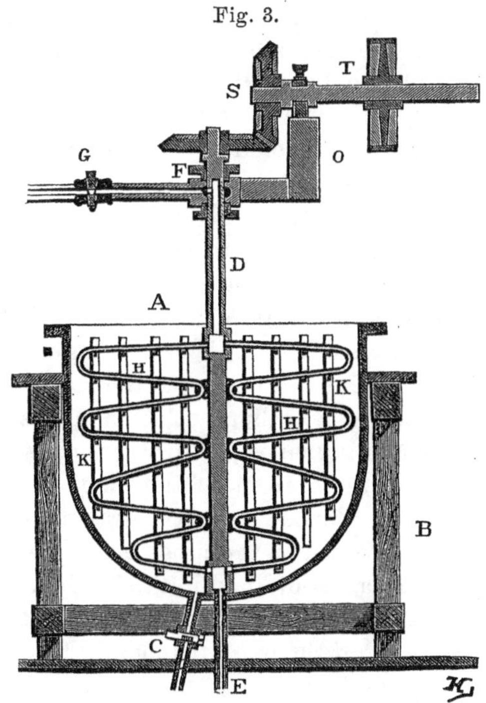

Fig. 3 represents a longitudinal vertical section of it. A is the soap-kettle, which can be made in any shape and of any material, having a draw-off faucet C, and mounted upon a frame B. D is an upright shaft, hollow both in its upper and lower parts, but solid in the middle. F is a box in which the shaft D runs, and provided with suitable packing and stuffing boxes and circular chamber, so that the steam arising from the pipe G can be admitted through openings in the hollow top part of the shaft D without leaking out of the box F. The lower end of the shaft D runs through the bottom of the kettle A, fitting sufficiently tight to prevent the soap and lye from running out, yet loose enough to be easily turned. Two, three, or four pipes H, so bent as to take the configuration of the kettle A, are connected at both ends with the hollow parts of the shaft D. K, K, K, are a number of slats fastened to the pipes H H, to strengthen them, and at the same time offer more resistance to the materials to be stirred. A set of gearings S, and a shaft T, mounted on the beam O, are so arranged as to give motion to the shaft D. The advantage derived from this arrangement is obvious, as the steam entering the pipe D finds no other outlet than the pipes H H, through which it rushes, following their sinuosities, till it reaches the bottom of the shaft D, where, re-entering, the condensed water is drawn off at E. The heat thus conveyed in the pipes H H is communicated to the materials contained in the kettle A, which being continually stirred, distribute the heat more uniformly throughout the mass than could be effected by the ordinary methods.

CHAPTER II.

OF POTASSA, SODA, AND CAUSTIC SODA.

POTASSA.

THIS alkali is called in commerce, vegetable alkali, sal tartar, pearlash, potash, and hydrated protoxide of potassium.

When the crude potash has been subjected to the heat of a reverberatory furnace, the product is termed pearlash. In commerce, it is found in solid hard pieces, interspersed sometimes with bluish, but oftener with reddish spots; oxide of iron, and a trace of sulphide of potassium, being the cause of the latter discoloration. The sal tartar is simply purified pearlash.

Potash itself is derived from certain plants, and especially from forest trees. These are cut down, converted into ashes and lixiviated. The liquid thus obtained is evaporated until it is brought to a solid state. This residue is subjected to the heat of a reverberatory furnace, for the purpose of drying it completely and freeing it from its sulphur and organic particles. In this state it is offered and sold in the market as pearlash. Plants and trees, however, are not the only sources from which it is derived, for it has recently been manufactured from certain crystalline rocks, from feldspar, for instance, which yields 17 per cent. of oxide of potassium, and about 5 per cent. is said to be producible from the New Jersey and Delaware green-sand.*

According to the species of plants and trees from which they are extracted, and the soil upon which those plants and trees grow, potashes contain a larger or smaller amount of carbonate of potassa (exclusively valuable to the savonnier) as well as of other substances, such as sulphate of potassa, chloride of potassium, carbonate, phosphate, and silicate of lime, the two first only being soluble in water. In addition to the carbonate of potassa, the American potash contains for the most part, caustic potassa. Ure found in the best pink Canadian potashes, almost uniformly, sixty per cent. of absolute potassa, and in the best pearlash fifty per cent.; the alkali of the former being nearly in a caustic state, but that of the latter carbonated.

Mayer of New York found in 100 parts of the American potash—

	1	2	3	4	5	6
Carbonate of alkali	43.6	24.5	15.0	56.0	53.1	38.47
Caustic alkali . .	49.6	44.4	38.6	5.6	4.4	....

* An analysis of a sample from Camden County, New Jersey, performed by G. T. Scattergood, has given the following result:

Insoluble silica	5.
Soluble silica	48.
Protoxide of iron	22.74
Alumina	6.61
Potassa	5.01
Soda	1.08
Lime	1.975
Magnesia	1.375
Phosphoric acid	4.821
Water	7.50
	99.611

Nos. 1, 2, and 4 were potashes of first quality; 3 and 5 were potashes of second, and No. 6 was potash of third quality. No. 2 yielded 15.8 per cent. of insoluble matter, and the amount of sulphate of alkali in No. 6 was as high as 53 per cent.

SODA.

Soda is of much more importance to the manufacturer of soap than potash, because he could not make the hard soap without it. It is found in a natural state on this continent, in Venezuela, and in Mexico, and when thus found it is called native soda. Urao is the term by which it is known in Mexico and in South America. The amount of native soda is, however, gradually decreasing, and totally inadequate to supply the proportionally increasing demand. A small fraction only of this surplus is derivable from the incineration of certain sea and shore plants, and by far the largest portion now used is acquired from the transformation of salt. The best quality of native soda, and most appreciated in this continent, is generally imported via England from Spain and the Levant, and known as barilla. It contains from fifteen to thirty per cent. of carbonate with a little sulphuret, and is mixed with sulphate and muriate of soda. Spanish sodas are very extensively used in England, being considered superior to the artificial, inasmuch as the hard soap is thereby found to be less brittle and more plastic, a peculiarity which in Ure's opinion is attributable to the small proportion of potassa which they always contain. Such sodas, moreover, and especially those extracted from plants, and possessing a considerable quantity of the chloride of sodium, were formerly exclusively used in the manufacture of the Marseilles olive oil soap during the salting operation, called by the French *relargage.* It was also further used in the second and third boiling. In lieu, however, of this kind, the salted soda,—the "*soude salée,*"—an artificial soda, is substituted in Marseilles, and is almost universally used at the present time; the method of manufacturing which, as has been previously remarked, is based upon the preparation of sulphate of soda from salt, its transformation into crude carbonate of soda (designated *black ash*), and the purification of the crude soda by lixiviation, evaporation, and calcination. The product thus obtained is termed *white ash*, or *soda ash.* According to Morfit, the standard of good soda-ash in our market is 80 per cent. carbonated, calculated both from caustic and carbonated soda.

Soda is found in commerce purer than potash, and mostly with uniform properties. Indeed, potash is often adulterated with it, owing to its cheapness. From the white soda ash, the soda salt, or the crystallized carbonate of soda, is produced, 100 parts of which consist of

Carbonate of soda	37.20
Water of crystallization	62.80

Caustic Soda.

It is only within the last few years that the caustic soda has been offered in the market, and can be purchased either as a solid or a liquid. In the latter state, it is denominated *concentrated lye*, and soapmakers find it a most convenient commodity, as it saves them the trouble of preparing it themselves. It is well known that a certain weight of caustic soda represents a larger amount of soda combining with the fats than the ordinary soda. We found it always nearly caustic.

Both red and white, of equal value, are in the market, but a prejudice exists against the former, the soapmakers being impressed with the idea that it is not so well adapted for their business as the latter. Their prejudices, however, are very groundless, for when the red caustic soda is dissolved, the coloring matter gradually settles at the bottom, and the liquid becomes entirely clear. In Europe they now use for making caustic soda, large quantities of a mineral called kryolithe, which is found in Greenland.

CHAPTER III.

ALKALIMETRY; OR, VALUATION OF THE COMMERCIAL SODA ASH, POTASSA, AND CAUSTIC SODA.

For the purpose of determining the value of the above alkalies, it is necessary to have—

A small hand-balance with weights, from one-half of a grain to 120 grains.

A glass mortar.

A set of test-tubes.

A glass spirit-lamp.

A (℥ii) flask.

A small evaporating dish of iron.

A small evaporating dish of porcelain.

A (℥i) glass funnel.

An iron tripod.

Litmus and filtering paper.

Necessary Chemicals.

Alcohol (ninety-five per cent.), ℥iv.

Nitric acid (pure), ℥ii.

Solution of chloride of barium, ℥ii.

Solution of nitrate of silver, ℥ii.

In order satisfactorily to estimate the commercial value of soda ash, or potash, or solid caustic soda, it is necessary to determine—

1st. The amount of water they contain.

2d. The amount of caustic and carbonated alkali.

3d. The foreign substances existing in them.

(1.) *Estimation of the Amount of Water.*—100 grs. of the alkali are heated in an iron capsule over a gas lamp, or other suitable heating apparatus, until all the water is expelled, which may be tested by a plate of cold glass or metal held for a moment over the capsule, when whatever vapor arises from the heated material will be condensed on its surface. After all the contained water is thus driven off, the loss of weight will indicate the amount of water existing in every 100 grs. of material, and the absolute weight of the desiccated parcel will be the per cent. of alkali contained in the crude material; the loss also will indicate the per cent. of water contained therein.

For example, if it weigh 90 grains, it obviously follows that, in the first instance, 10 per cent. of the whole consisted of water.

(2.) *Estimation of the Amount of Caustic and Carbonated Alkali.*—In a given sample, it is very important to ascertain if we have only caustic alkali or only carbonated alkali, as well as the amount of each it contains. For example, if we have a potash or soda, of which only one-third is caustic, and two-thirds carbonated alkali, the latter amount must be changed into the caustic state before it can be used in soapmaking. It is best, we would observe, first to determine the amount of caustic alkali.

(*a.*) *Estimation of the Amount of Caustic Alkali.*—Concentrated alcohol, it must be remembered, will only dissolve caustic soda, and not in any way affect the other ingredients always found in commercial potash, soda, or caustic soda. Hence, if we take 50 grains of commercial soda, reduce them to powder in a glass mortar, put half of it in a two-ounce flask, with the addition of half an ounce of alcohol of 95 per cent., shaken all well together, and leaving it stand for a few hours, afterwards transfer the liquid floating on the top carefully into an evaporating capsule of porcelain, and let it quickly evaporate over a lamp, gradually increasing the temperature until nothing more evaporates, and then when cooled, immediately weigh the capsule again, we thereby ascertain the actual amount of caustic soda which the sample contains. If, for example, the product be 20 grains, it consequently follows that in the original 100 grains of commercial soda, 40 per cent. is composed of caustic soda. Before, however, the evaporating process is commenced, in order that nothing be lost, a little alcohol should be mixed with the deposit in the flask, and being filtered, added to the liquid which had already been transferred.

(*b.*) *Estimation of the Amount of Carbonated Alkali: (Indirect).*—In this process, it is requisite to determine, first, the actual amount of alkali existing in the soda or potash, and this being ascertained, the quantity of carbonated alkali is reduced by calculation.

50 grains of the alkaline sample are to be dissolved in a flask containing two ounces of water. Next weigh out, on a watch-glass, 100 grains of well-crystallized oxalic acid, reduced to a fine powder. Small portions of this acid powder are then to be added at a time (by means of a spatula or knife) to the alkaline solution, shaking the liquid between

each addition, or stirring it with a glass rod, heating and testing it with litmus paper, till the latter becomes slightly reddened, while the liquid is hot. The residue of the oxalic acid is then weighed, and supposing it to be 43 grains, it is obvious that to saturate the alkali in the 50 grains of the sample, 57 grains of oxalic acid were consumed.

Now 7.87 grains of oxalic acid are capable of saturating or removing the alkaline reaction of 5 grains of caustic soda, or 7 grains of caustic potassa.

Suppose the alkali we have thus analyzed be a sample of soda ash in which we have already ascertained the amount of caustic soda, then the whole amount of alkali we have now found in the 50 grains is calculated upon caustic soda.

$$\frac{57 \times 5}{7.87} = 36.2.$$

But we found under (*a*) by direct determination, that the real amount of caustic soda in 50 grains = 20 grains. Then 16.2 grains (the difference between 36.2 and 20), are to be calculated upon carbonate of soda. As now 5 grains of caustic soda are equivalent to 6.62 grains of carbonate of soda,* 16.2 caustic soda are, therefore, equivalent to 21.5 grains of carbonate of soda. This is 43 per cent.

We have hitherto found in the respective soda ash: water, 10 per cent.; caustic soda, 40 per cent.; carbonate of soda, 43 per cent. Hence, assuming these results to be accurate, the amount of foreign substances in the sample of soda ash is 7 per cent.

---

* 7 grains of caustic potassa are equivalent to 8.63 carbonate of potassa.

(*c.*) *Determination of the Nature of Foreign Ingredients.*—These may be soluble or insoluble. As they are not taken up by the lye, the savonnier cares little or nothing about the insoluble substances; but in some cases he is interested in those which are soluble, though they are not of any value for him. Generally they are found to be chlorides or sulphates. The former are detected by adding a solution of nitrate of silver to a clear solution of the substance to be examined, which has been previously slightly acidulated with chemically pure nitric acid, and if there be chloride of potassium or salt present, a white curdy precipitate will be formed, which, by exposure to light, becomes first violet, and subsequently black.

Sulphates, on the other hand, are detected by first neutralizing the solution with nitric acid and then adding a solution of chloride of barium, a finely pulverulent heavy white precipitate is formed.

To many it may be of interest, if not of importance, to ascertain, moreover, if there be any sulphide of sodium,* because, for instance, a potash or soda containing such, would be unfit for the manufacture of white soap. Its presence, indeed, will have been already indicated by the development of hydrosulphuric acid, by adding an acid to a solution of the alkali, a gas very much resembling rotten eggs in its smell. But where the odor of the gas fails to afford sufficient proof of the presence of hydrosulphuric acid, the application of the following reagent will remove

---

* This ingredient is often detected in the potash and soda, but never in the caustic soda.

all doubt. The air suspected to contain it, is tested by placing in it a small slip of paper, moistened with a solution of acetate of lead, and if the gas be present, the slip becomes covered with a thin, brownish-black, shining film of sulphide of lead.

CHAPTER IV.

OF THE PREPARATION OF THE LYES.

Of the Water.—Only spring or river water should be used in making soap, which, moreover, must be perfectly clear, otherwise clear lye cannot be produced. It must also be free from organic matters, for these are often dissolved, and though imperceptible, soon cause the water to become putrid. Nearly all waters contain mineral matters in solution. Hard waters, for instance, contain a certain amount of carbonate of lime, gypsum, chloride of calcium, and magnesium. When such waters are used, though the lyes be equally good, and the process of saponification not impeded, still there will be a loss of material in proportion to the quantity of alkali neutralized. A water containing more than twelve grains of such substances in one gallon, should be rejected. If hard water be used in soapboiling, the *quality* is not injuriously affected (as in dyeing), nor, we repeat, does it retard the process (as is the case in brewing, for such waters act against fermentation). But it is, for the above-mentioned reason, a good plan, to make a careful examination of a certain kind of water before using it. For such cases, the services of a chemist will be required.

Preparation of the Lyes.

Lye is an aqueous solution of caustic soda or potassa, and by the agency of which the chemical decomposition of the fat and its conversion to soap are effected. Caustic soda, indeed, is at present a commercial commodity, but it may occasionally happen that the savonnier will have to prepare his own lyes from the carbonates, especially the potassa. Hence the expediency, in our opinion, of describing the

Fig. 4.

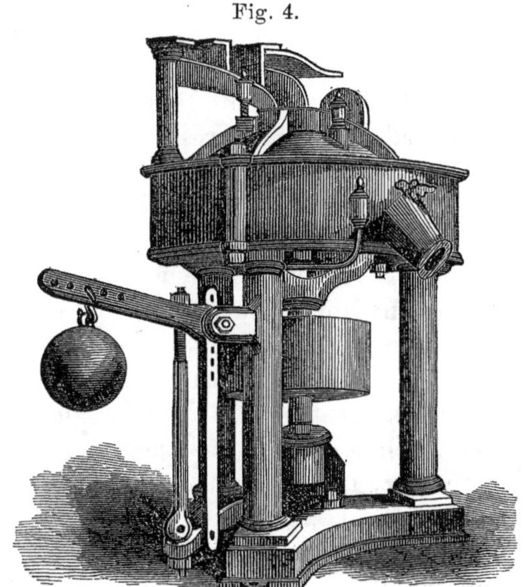

Bogardus Eccentric Mill, for the reduction of the alkalies.

method by means of which lyes can be prepared. They can be prepared in two ways. One plan is to reduce the soda or potassa into pieces about the size of a nut, mix it with slacked lime, let it stand twenty-four hours, and then leach it out with water. For this purpose, they have in France tanks of brick-work or sheet-iron, capable of holding from two hundred to five hundred gallons, and having a perforated floor, placed from two to four inches above the bottom, and covered with a layer of straw, on which is poured the mixture of lime with the alkali. A faucet is inserted between this perforated floor and the bottom, by means of which the liquor can be drawn off. The lyes prepared in this way are called "lessives faites à froid," but these are never perfectly caustic; whilst in this process, though possibly the most convenient, more lime is requisite than when the following method is adopted, which results in the formation of perfectly caustic soda. The potash or soda (not too concentrated a solution), should be thoroughly brought together with lime-milk, this process being sustained with heat. The carbonic acid of the alkalies thus uniting with the lime, forms insoluble carbonate of lime, which settles at the bottom. We stated above, that the solution of the alkalies must not be too strong; it moreover must be of a definite concentration. A French chemist, for instance, ascertained that it was necessary that there should not be more than fifteen per cent. of alkali in the solution, otherwise there would remain a portion of the carbonated alkali undecomposed.

Suppose one hundred pounds of pearlash have to be transformed into caustic potash; for this purpose, a one hundred and fifty gallon kettle, containing eighty-five gallons of water, should be heated with steam or open fire; and when it boils, the pearlash, having been previously pulverized, should be gradually dropped in, stirring it all the time. As soon as it is thus dissolved, forty-eight pounds of *slacked* lime, made into milk of lime, should also be gradually put into this boiling liquor. Experience has proved, that for the thorough decomposition of the carbonates of the alkalies, the process of boiling must be continuous and uninterrupted, and the lime of a milky consistency, not in pieces, nor in powder.

In order to ascertain whether the lye is caustic or not, take a test-glass full, let it stand till cool, then filter, and drop into the clear liquid some nitric acid; if it effervesce, the lye is not caustic, and *vice versâ;* when not caustic, the boiling has to be continued till the portion taken from the kettle shows, when filtered, no escape of carbonic acid, if nitric acid be added. As soon as no carbonic acid escapes from the lye, thus tested, the fire should be taken out, the liquor carefully covered, and suffered to remain undisturbed for twelve or fifteen hours, so that the lime may settle. After this, the clear liquor should be transferred by a syphon into a wooden vat, lined inside with sheet lead, and having a cullendered false bottom, and cock fitted near the bottom (see Fig. 5), so that the clear lye may be drawn off.

The number of vats necessary, depends, of course, on the amount of business transacted, each of which should be kept carefully covered. The remainder in the kettle, containing yet some lye, may be lixiviated two or three times with water, for though weaker lyes are thereby thus obtained, they are nevertheless serviceable at times.

The lime used must be of a good quality, and not

been exposed to the atmosphere. *Fat* lime is best; only the quantity actually required should be slacked at a time, because the hydrate of lime (as well as the lyes) loses its causticity when exposed to the air.

Fig. 5.

For one hundred pounds of crystallized soda, twenty-four pounds of quicklime are requisite; for one hundred pounds of pearlash, double that quantity (or forty-eight pounds), and for one hundred pounds of soda ash, sixty pounds will generally be required.* We may however observe, that for the transformation of pearlash or soda into caustic lyes, more or less quicklime is necessary, according to the amount of carbonated alkalies they contain. For instance, if the

* As concerns the quantity of the lime mentioned here, it is one-fifth more than would be necessary according to the calculation.

pearlash contains only seventy per cent. of carbonate,

$$\frac{70\times48}{100}=33.6 \text{ pounds}$$

of lime will be necessary, for one hundred pounds of pearlash; a surplus of lime, however, we may observe, never proves injurious.

Estimation of the Strength of the Lyes.

For this purpose Baumé's hydrometer, with which almost every soapmaker is acquainted, is generally used, though it does not always indicate the true strength of the lyes, because in dividing the stem, a perfectly pure lye of caustic alkali is used, whereas that now employed by the savonnier never is pure, but contains always the peculiar impurities of the soda or potash (sulphates and chlorides). These influence the specific weight of the lyes. As, for instance, a lye in which the alkalimeter indicates eighteen per cent. of caustic alkali, does not really contain eighteen per cent. of pure caustic alkali, but includes also the foreign matters. This is especially the case in weak lyes, more so than in strong. When using this instrument, therefore, we must bear in mind, that it gives us only the indications of the relative strength of the lyes.

The following table exhibits the quantity of fused potassa and solid caustic soda in 100 parts of lye, with their respective degrees, after Baumé's hydrometer:

Degrees.	Specific Gravity.	Potassa in 100.	Soda in 100.
40°	1.357	33.46	32.40
35°	1.299	29.34	28.16
30°	1.245	24.77	22.58
25°	1.196	20.30	17.71
20°	1.151	16.40	13.77
18°	1.134	14.38	12.
16°	1.117	12.29	10.26
14°	1.101	10.59	8.85
12°	1.085	9.20	7.69
10°	1.070	7.74	6.49
8°	1.055	6.25	5.46
6°	1.041	4.77	4.02
4°	1.027	3.21	2.92
2°	1.013	1.63	1.38
0°	1.0	——	——

In certain cases, it is requisite to transform stronger lyes into weaker of a definite degree of strength. Though, to effect this, much precision is needed; still, we think the reader will find little, if any difficulty, after perusing the annexed part, containing four tables for the reduction of strong lyes, published by Mr. Eugène Lormé, the excellent author of the work "Manuel complet du Savonnier."

The first column at the left of each table shows the quantity and the degree of the lye to be diluted.

The second indicates the quantity of water to be added to the lye.

The third gives the amount of the lye obtained by the admixture of both liquids; and

The fourth exhibits the areometric degree of the lye.

TABLE I.

Showing the different areometric degrees resulting from a mixture of 10 *gallons of soda lye, of* 36 *degrees Baumé, with quantities of water varying from* 10 *to* 90 *gallons.*

Number of gallons of Lye of 36 degrees.	Number of gallons of Water.	Number of gallons of obtained Lye.	Areometric degree of the Lye.
10	10	20	23
10	20	30	17
10	30	40	14
10	40	50	12
10	50	60	10
10	60	70	9
10	70	80	8
10	80	90	7¼
10	90	100	6¾

10 gallons of lye, of 36 degrees Baumé, weigh 112½ lbs.

TABLE II.

Showing the different areometric degrees resulting from a mixture of 10 *lbs. of soda lye, of* 36 *degrees Baumé, with quantities of water varying from* 10 *to* 100 *lbs.*

Number of pounds of Lye of 36 degrees.	Number of pounds of Water to be employed.	Number of pounds of Lye obtained.	Areometric degree of the Lye.
10	10	20	21
10	20	30	14½
10	30	40	11½
10	40	50	10
10	50	60	9
10	60	70	8
10	70	80	6½
10	80	90	5½
10	90	100	5 nearly.

8.8 gallons of lye, of 30 degrees Baumé, weigh 100 lbs.

TABLE III.

Showing the different areometric degrees resulting from a mixture of 10 gallons of soda lye, of 30 degrees Baumé, with quantities of water varying from 10 to 90 gallons.

Number of gallons of Lye of 30 degrees.	Number of gallons of Water to be employed.	Number of gallons of Lye obtained.	Areometric degree of the Lye.
10	10	20	19
10	20	30	nearly 14
10	30	40	11
10	40	50	9
10	50	60	8
10	60	70	7
10	70	80	6
10	80	90	5
10	90	100	4½

Remarks.—10 gallons of soda lye, of 30 degrees, weigh 104 lbs.; 75 gallons of this lye and 25 gallons of water give 100 gallons of lye of 25 degrees Baumé. There are 23¼ lbs. of caustic soda wanted for making 10 gallons of lye of 30 degrees Baumé.

TABLE IV.

Showing the different areometric degrees resulting from a mixture of 10 lbs. of soda lye, of 30 degrees Baumé, with quantities of water varying from 10 to 90 lbs.

Number of pounds of Lye of 30 degrees.	Number of pounds of Water to be employed.	Number of pounds of Lye obtained.	Areometric degree of the Lye.
10	10	20	17
10	20	30	12
10	30	40	9½
10	40	50	7½
10	50	60	6½
10	60	70	5½
10	70	80	5 or 5¼
10	80	90	4½
10	90	100	4

9.6 gallons of lye, of 30 degrees Baumé, weigh 100 pounds.

CHAPTER V.

SAPONIFIABLE FATS.

Nature of Fats.

All the naturally occurring fats are mixtures of substances, the constituents of which are similar to the salts which inorganic chemistry embodies, *i. e.*, we find in the fats several organic acids and bases. For instance, the sulphate of soda, or the glauber salt (in daily use) is the combination of an acid (the sulphuric acid) with a base (the soda). The fats are, similarly, combinations of acids (the fatty acids), with a base (the fat base). The difference between the constitution of an inorganic salt (as above described), and those of fats, is simply this: in the former there is only *one* base with *one* acid, in the latter several fatty acids are united with one base, whilst others also have several bases.

The most common fat base is the *oxide of glyceril* (with which we are unacquainted in its pure state), but which we know unites with water immediately after its separation from the other constituents of the fats, and thus forms the *glycerine*, or *sweet principle of oils.* In the salting operation, this glycerine sinks below the lye, and becomes dissolved in the brine.

The most common fatty acids are: the margaric, the stearic, and the oleic, which, uniting with the oxide of glyceril, form the margarine, the stearine, and the oleine, of which, in various proportions, all fats consist. The margarine is found principally in the butters, and not drying vegetable oils, the stearine in the suets, and the olein constitutes the liquid portion of most animal and many vegetable fats; in these latter, too, palmitin, another principle, and somewhat resembling margarine, is sometimes traceable, especially in the palm oil. The palm oil has also this additional peculiarity, that it contains *free* acids, the quantity of which increases with its age, and hence the reason why old palm oil saponifies better than fresh. Pelouze and Boudet found in one sample of fresh palm oil, one-third free acid, in another, one and a half, and in a third, nearly four-fifths of its weight.

There are, moreover, found in fats, tissues, albumen, traces of slime, pigments, and often peculiar acids, which impart to them a peculiar odor.

In regard to the mutton and goose fat, Chevreul has proved that they owe their strong and penetrating odor to a peculiar substance which he calls hircine.

Having thus made, as we think, some necessary remarks on the immediate principle and nature of the fats, we proceed to a special consideration of the various fats, and first we will speak of the

Vegetable Fats or Oils.

They have generally a very different consistency; some remain liquid at a temperature of +5 to +4° F., some, as the olive oil, solidify at the freezing-point of water, whilst others coagulate at a temperature of

50° to 60° F., as is the case with the palm oil and cocoanut oil; these are also called butters.

All the oils, with few exceptions, are lighter than water; their specific gravity oscillates between 0.919 and 0.9 of 0. They, however, have many properties in common, as, for instance, they are both liquid at a temperature of 65° to 85° F., and both insoluble in cold and hot water, but easily soluble in ether, and all of a sweet taste.

Exposed to the atmosphere for some time, many undergo remarkable changes. Some solidify, others thicken and become hard, but retain their brilliancy. Vegetable oils have consequently been divided into two classes, into the drying or siccative, and into the fluid or non-siccative oils. Of the first named, are oil of linseed, hempseed, and poppy oil. Of the second, olive oil, palm oil, sweet almonds, and cocoanut oil.

According to the mode of obtaining oils, we distinguish oils of the first and second pressure. Experience has shown that those of the second pressure are more serviceable to the soap manufacturer, for though less liquid and often mucilaginous, they nevertheless contain more stearine, and we must remember the richer the oils are in stearine, the harder are the soaps they yield.

Cocoanut Oil.

This substance, also called cocoanut butter, is found in a liquid state in the nut of some palm species, growing in Brazil, Ceylon, and at the coasts of Malabar and Bengal. In commerce, the nut is called "copperah;" it yields sixty per cent. of the fatty substance. The cocoa butter is white, sweet, and of the consistency of lard, of a mild taste, and when fresh, of an agreeable odor. Its melting-point lies between 60° and 70° F., and it becomes easily rancid.

Six different fatty acids have been discovered in the cocoa butter, most of which being solids, accounts for the great firmness of the soaps it forms. This fat is also remarkable in another relation, uniting with soda lyes in any proportion, without separating from them. Owing to this exceptional property, this fat is used in large quantities for the making of filled soaps. It is very slow to unite with lye by itself; it is therefore usually applied in combination with tallow or palm oil, increasing their emollient properties, and also giving to the tallow soaps a brilliant whiteness.

Palm Oil.

This fat, which owing to its consistency, should more properly be called palm butter, is obtained from the fruit of several varieties of palm trees, growing especially in South America, at the western coast of Africa, and in the East Indies. The Canary Islands and Madeira, also furnish us palm oil. The commercial oil never is identical in its composition, which difference probably must be ascribed to the state of maturity of the fruits, and especially to the varieties of the trees from which the oils are extracted. The palm butter is of an orange color, and when not rancid, of a violet odor. The commercial kinds have different denominations; the *prima lagos* and *secunda lagos* are considered the best. The melting-point of the fresh crude palm butter, is, according to Payen, at 80° F., while it is of a much higher fusing-point when old. In commerce, we find sometimes a fictitious article, which is nothing more than tallow and lard melted together, colored with natural palm oil and aromatized with powdered orris root. This article, however, is easily distinguished from the natural palm oil, for the genuine is soluble in acetic ether, whilst the spurious will not dissolve.

Palm oil is employed both in the bleached and in the natural state. In the bleached state it produces a soap of most beautiful whiteness, and rich with the characteristic odor of the oil, especially when the oil is operated upon by the chromic acid process, which we propose to describe hereafter.

For the bleaching of 1000 lbs. there is necessary 5 lbs. red chromate of potassa, 10 lbs. strong hydrochloric acid, and 2½ lbs. sulphuric acid. First, the chromate of potassa is pulverized and solved in hot water (twenty pounds of water will be enough to effect solution). The palm oil should next be transferred in a wooden tank, and heated with steam until 120° F. are reached; this temperature obtained, the steam is turned off and a portion of the solution of the chromate of potassa is added, agitated, and a proportional portion of hydrochloric acid added; at last the sulphuric acid. After thoroughly agitating this mixture with the oil for a few minutes, the oil changes in color, becoming first black, then dark green (of the resulting oxide of chromium), and soon afterwards light green, when a thick froth appears on the surface, which appearance is an indication of the completion of the process. If a sample of the oil, when taken out and allowed to settle, does not appear sufficiently decolorized, an additional portion of the bichromate of potassa, with muriatic and sulphuric acids, should be added. The process is completed in from twenty to thirty minutes.

The whole has to be left quiet for one hour, so that the solution of the resulting salts may settle. The clear oil is then drawn off in a wooden cask, mixed with some water, and heated again by the introduction of steam. It is again left alone for some time, and the fat subsequently drawn off.

In making soaps palm oil is usually employed with tallow, in the proportion of twenty to thirty of the former to one hundred of the latter. It is also usually employed in making rosin soap in order to correct the flavor of the rosin and brighten the color.

Olive Oil

is procured from France, Spain, Portugal, Italy, Greece, Northern Africa, and from the islands of the Mediterranean. It seems to have been known from antiquity, for its mode of manufacture is mentioned in holy writ, and what is remarkable it has but little varied since. We distinguish particularly three kinds of oils, namely: the oil of the first pressure, or virgin oil (*huile fine on vierge*) obtained by a gentle pressure of the freshly gathered fruit; a second kind is gained by submitting them, when thus pressed, to the action of hot water and pressing them between metallic plates previously heated; and the third inferior kind (called *les ressences*) is the product of this residuum, or *marc*, when boiled in water. Only these two latter kinds serve in the manufacture of soaps; often they are adulterated with cheaper oils. In the order of the affinity of the fatty bodies to the alkalies the olive oil occupies the first rank; it yields, also, a very excellent soap, highly estimated for its fresh and agreeable odor. It is very extensively used by soap manufactories in Marseilles and for the well-known Windsor soap. An old receipt prescribes nine parts of good ox tallow and one part of olive oil. There is very little demand for it in this country, probably owing to its costliness, and it is seldom used, except in the limited manufacture of the finest toilet soap.

Oil of Poppy.

This name is given to the product, on pressure, of the bruised seed of the *Papaver somniferus*. It is whitish-yellow, inodorous, of an almond taste, and when pure less viscous than most oils, and remains liquid even to 0° F. It belongs to the class of drying oils. Seeds of poppy are brought from the East Indies to some extent for oils. It is especially used for the manufacture of soft soaps; and in France it is employed with tallow for the manufacture of an imitation Marseilles soap.

Galam Butter.

In addition to the above-described fats, we will mention three fatty bodies, of the consistency of tallow, which have lately been brought into the English market.

The galam butter is the product of the *Bassia butyracea*, a tree growing in Africa. It is of a reddish-white color, mild odor and taste, and saponifies readily. It has been found to contain eighty-two per cent. of stearine, and eighteen per cent. of oleine, and is solid at 85° F. Another fatty substance, met with in Africa very often by travellers, is obtained from the *butter tree* of Shea; it was discovered by Mungo Park.

Stillingia Butter

is a fat exported from China, and obtained by pressure from the fruit of a tree growing in the valley of Chusan. It is of a brilliant whiteness, of little or no odor, harder than the common tallow, and fuses at 99° F. As to the method of obtaining it, and from what part of the tree it is extracted, various and very opposite opinions are entertained.

Mafurra Tallow

is a newly-discovered fatty matter, extracted by hot water from the mafurra kernel; these kernels are of the size of a cacao bean, which abound in Mozambique, Madagascar, and the Isle of Reunion. It has a yellowish color, and an odor similar to that of cocoa butter. It is less fusible than tallow, and with the alkalies forms a brown soap. It contains a large percentage of solid fat, and it is said to be easily procurable at a cheap rate.

Animal Fats.

Though identical in their elementary composition with vegetable fats, they are nevertheless distinguishable by their color, odor, and consistency, as well as by the larger proportion of stearine and margarine they contain. It is to these constituents that the animal fats owe their solidity. There is, however, also a great difference in the consistency of the animal fats, whilst the richer they are in solid constituents, the higher is their melting-point. In the Cetacei, a class of whale fishes, the fats are generally fluid; in the carnivorous animals soft and rank-flavored; and nearly scentless in the ruminants; usually white and copious in well-fed young animals; yellowish and more scanty in the old. The degree of firmness, moreover, is not the same in all parts of the organism. The fat of the kidneys is generally harder and more compact than that found in the cellular tissues and in the bowels of animals. In general, the fat of the female is softer than that of the male, easily perceptible, as the tallow of the ox compared with that of the cow. Even the climate has its influences, for we find that in the temperate zone, the fats have greater hardness, and are more compact than those of colder countries; the same may be said of the seasons, as we find that the fat of animals killed during the summer months is much softer than that of animals killed during the winter. The nourishment, also, has a marked and material influence; for the dryer, more substantial, colder the fodder, the better and harder will be the fat. Oil cakes and distillery slops diminish the consistency of it.

The color and odor of the fats have, of course, effect in the manufacture of soaps; but interesting and useful as these details are, we are obliged to abridge them, and pass to a more special consideration of the fats.

Beef Tallow.

Of all animal fats, this is the most used. Its general characters are well known; it has a yellowish tint, due to a peculiar coloring matter, separable by several washings in hot water, and is firm, brittle, but not so white as mutton suet. That rendered by steam, as is now universally done in France, is generally the whitest. The melting-point of beef tallow we found to be as high as 111° F., and it can be cooled down to 102° F. before it becomes solid again. Among the varieties of tallow which appear in commerce, the North American is the most in demand (it contains about seventy per cent. of stearine). The Russian tallow is also much esteemed; less so the tallow from South America.

Mutton Suet.

Mutton suet is generally compact, firm, whiter, and has less odor than beef tallow; however, when the fat is stale the smell is most disagreeable and nauseating. Mutton fat, moreover, is richer in stearine than beef tallow, and is consequently much sought after by the tallow as well as the stearine candle manufacturers. Saponified with soda lye it yields a beautiful white soap, but being so rich in stearine it is liable to become too hard and brittle. In order, therefore, to obtain a milder and more unctuous product it is generally mixed with fifteen to twenty per cent. of lard or cocoanut oil, whereby a superior soap is obtained, especially adapted as stock for the manufacture of toilet soaps.

Hog Fat (Lard).

This is generally prepared from the adipose matter of the omentum and mesentery of the hog, by freeing it from the membranous matter connected with it, washing with water and melting it with moderate heat, so as to separate the fat from the cracklings. In this state it is an important article of trade. Western lard is generally rendered by steam; it has also a granular appearance, and can be pressed for oil without any further granulation. Corn-fed lard has the most consistency, made-fed is next in quality, while that obtained from hogs, fed on distillery refuse, is thin, flabby, and deficient in body. Lard has, when fresh, a mild and agreeable taste, the consistency of butter, and its melting-point is at 81° F. It consists of sixty-two per cent. liquid fat or oleine, and thirty-eight per cent. of solid fat. When granulated and pressed at a low temperature, it yields a fluid, denominated lard oil, which, as a commercial commodity, varies materially in quality. The pressed cake, consisting chiefly of stearine, is termed *solar stearine*, and exclusively used in the manufacture of candles. Lard is an excellent material for soap manufacturers; it forms a white, sweet, and pure soap. For the purpose of rendering it more frothing it is saponified either with tallow or cocoanut oil.

Horse Fat

is found in trade from a white to a brown color; it is mostly extracted by steam from different parts of dead horses, and there are from fifty to one hundred pounds obtained from one horse. The soap made from horse fat, after several successive boilings, is white and firm; but owing to its peculiar odor it can only be employed advantageously in the preparation of demi-palm and rosin soap.

Bone Fat.

Bones contain, on an average, about five per cent. of fat, brownish-white in color, and of an oily consistency. Only fresh bones are adapted for the extraction of fat, because when bones are kept for some time, the fat permeates the texture of the bones in such a manner as to render its extraction very difficult. Where no machinery is used, the bones are generally split up lengthways by a hatchet, boiled in water, by means of which the fat is evolved, decanted, and filtered.

For purifying and deodorizing bone fat, Mr. H. Schwarz recommends to melt the fat and a small quantity of saltpetre together, and afterwards add a sufficiency of sulphuric acid, to decompose the latter. The mass scums very much, becomes of a light yellow color, loses its noxious smell entirely, and furnishes a fat very well adapted for soaps.

Fish Oil

is a term applied to various products very different in their origin. The fat of several species of whales, for instance, is employed to obtain fish oil, such as the cachalot, the pot-fish, the whale of Greenland, the Antarctic whale (*Balena Australis*), different dolphin species, the narvall, the sea-porc, and several species of robben and mammifera belonging to the class of whales. According to the origin, consequently, there are different kinds of fish oil in the market. The oil, for instance, which flows out spontaneously from the fat heaped up in a reservoir, is called white fish oil. There are also boiled fish oils, and, under the name of *train oil*, a variety of inferior qualities are included. For their further purification, bone-black is often mixed with them, and after remaining a month or two they are filtered through charcoal. The chemical composition of fish oil is very complicated, as it contains volatile odors, acids, gall, and different salts. Fish oil is used as a burning fluid, for making soft soaps, and adulterating other oils, and by the manufacturers of chamois leather.

Sperm Oil and Spermaceti.

In the head and special cavities of the cranium of several Cetacei, especially of the pot-fish or cachalot, and some species of dolphins, there is a liquid fat from which, after the death of the animal, a large quantity of a white, firm, tallow-like substance is separated. The liquid part is what is called sperm oil, and the solid part spermaceti. The sperm oil is found in commerce bleached and unbleached, the latter having a brownish appearance and disagreeable odor; chemically regarded, it is very interesting. It is easily saponified and the soap resulting is readily solved in water. The spermaceti is almost exclusively used for luxus candles.

Oleic Acid.

Though no animal fat, but occurring from such, we will say a few words on it in addition to the above-described fats. *Oleic acid* or *red oil* is a product incidental to the manufacture of adamantine candles. There are two kinds in commerce. The one formed by the process of distillation is only fit for making soft soap, owing to its disagreeable odor, whilst the other, the result of simple pressure, yields soaps of great consistency, whether saponified alone or with an admixture of tallow or other fats. In cool weather, oleic acid has a mushy consistency, attributable to the solidification of the solid fat which it reduces from the stearine cakes, and amounts to ten or fifteen per cent. It often contains a small amount of sulphuric acid, hence, it should be borne in mind, that oleic acid ought to be washed with some weak lye before using it. It is not only employed by soapmakers, but also by other manufacturers, and is therefore an article very much in demand.

Elaidic Acid.

By the action of hyponitric acid upon oleic acid, a pearly white, crystalline substance is obtained, of the consistence of tallow, and termed elaidic acid. It is manufactured on a large scale in England, since it has been found that it is equally serviceable to both soap and candle manufacturers.

PART II.

ON THE MANUFACTURE OF SOAP.

THE MANUFACTURE OF SOAP.

CHAPTER I.

ON THE BOILING OF SOAP.

1. The Paste or Preliminary Operation.

(*Vorsieden.*)

The purpose of this operation is to produce a preliminary combination of fat and lye. This is done in very different ways. Some soapmakers use during the whole operation a lye of the same strength, while others commence with a weak lye, then use one of middle strength, and finish with a strong one. In the first case, a lye is employed of 10 to 15° B. In the second, of 7 to 10, 15 to 18, and 18 to 25° B., successively. In some cases, as in the manufacture of red oil soap, very strong lyes are employed, say of 25 to 30° B.; usually the fat is first put in the pan and then the lye is added. For the paste operation, no lyes should be used containing foreign salts (such as are found in inferior kinds of soda), for then it is very difficult to form a union of the fats with the lye, and no good sud is obtained. But when the soap has been separated from the lye by salt, lyes containing salt may be used. In saponifying red oil, salty lyes may also be employed from the beginning. It is in all operations, however, a chief condition that the lye be caustic, because carbonate of soda (at least under ordinary pressure and temperature), will never decompose fat, *i. e.*, it will not unite with it.

For transforming one hundred pounds of fat into soap, about fourteen pounds of caustic soda are necessary, but generally more is employed, because the soda used in this country is never a pure hydrate of soda. In France, more lye is used for the paste operation than elsewhere, because the waste lye is employed over and over again, and consequently there is no loss. The saponification, moreover, is thus perfect and more easily performed.

The quantity of lye taken is also differently regulated by the manufacturers. Some add in the beginning the whole amount of lye, others add it gradually and in small quantities. This last mode is, in any case, preferable; for a great quantity of lye added at once will never act so energetically upon the fat as one might suppose *à priori.* Water retards saponification, inasmuch as the resulting soap, being insoluble in the strong lye, forms a smeary mass, that surrounds the non-decomposed fat, separates it, and thus impedes the action of the lye upon the fat. But when about one-fourth of the lye, in the beginning, is added, it soon forms with the fat a milky liquid or emulsion, which in heating gradually becomes clearer, producing a transparent soap solution, with intermingled fat drops. From time to time, in order to test it, a drop of the paste should be put on the tip of the tongue, when, if there still be free alkali in it, a burning sensation will be produced, in which case the boiling must be continued until a sweetish taste is experienced. More lye should then be added, under constant stirring, until the entire quantity is consumed. In this stage of the operation, the contents of the kettle are transformed into a homogeneous, clear liquid, in which we can discover neither lye nor fat. If, moreover, the liquid be *perfectly* clear, it shows that the right proportion of fat and lye has been applied. Should saponification progress too slowly, a weak lye of from 1 to 2° B. may be added, and even soap scraps will facilitate the combination of the fat with the alkali. By heating with an open fire, it sometimes happens that a portion of the paste, when it thickens, attaches itself to the bottom of the vessel, becomes overheated and burns. This burning is indicated by a black smoke passing off here and there with the vapor. When this occurs, the fire should forthwith be reduced, and some gallons of the strongest lye added to prevent further mischief. By these means a slight separation of the soap from the lye is occasioned, and the contact between the former and the metallic surface destroyed. In all cases, however, the paste operation will be complete, when, having taken out the stirring-rod, the paste no longer *drops* from it, but slides down in long threads. This appearance is called "spinning" of the soap.

We next pass on to the second operation, *i. e.*, to the separation of the soap from the under lye, technically denominated "cutting up the pan."

2. Cutting up the Pan.

(*Aussalzen.*)

This is done by stirring into the ingredients of the soap-kettle, either soda lye, containing salt, or a solution of salt, or dry salt. The separation in all these cases is founded upon the insolubility of the soap in brine or *strong* caustic lyes, whereas *weak* lyes would dissolve it. Of all soaps, the cocoanut-oil soap is the most remarkable, for, being dissolved by a brine solution, it is peculiarly serviceable for washing in salt water, whence its name, "*marine soap.*" This soap becomes so hard, that when separated from the glycerine, it cannot be cut with a knife, and consequently the salting operation should not be performed, but the soap boiled in strong lye with one water.

The following is the method by which the salting operation is effected: one workman gradually adds the brine or dry salt, while another agitates the paste with a stirring rod *from below upwards.* This is done under gentle boiling. It is also essential to add the salt in the right proportion, the effect of which is not immediate but gradual, so that the whole amount requisite should not be stirred in at once, but in portions of about one-sixth. After half of it has been dropped in, the soap should be allowed to boil for about ten minutes before any addition is made. Acerding to concentration, twelve to sixteen pounds of salt are necessary for one hundred pounds of fat, in order to separate the formed soap from the surplus of water. The separation is perfect, when the aqueous portion is observed to run off from the curdy mass; when a sample is taken with a spatula, it is not of an adhesive character whilst hot; and when, on placing some in the palm of the hand, and rubbing it with the thumb, it hardens into firm scales. The termination of the process is furthermore indicated when the surface splits up into several fields, separated from each other by deep furrows, in which there is not the fresh and soft appearance of froth, but of dry slabs, which, being forced from side to side by the escaping vapor, slowly arrange themselves one above the other.

The fire should be extinguished when the soap, which was always covered with froth and bubbles, suddenly sinks and the froth breaks up into roundish massive grains, distinctly separated from each other and from the saline solution. The salting being completed, the mass should be suffered to remain quiet for several hours, and then the under-lye drawn off by the faucet.

3. Clear-Boiling.

(Klarsieden.)

In this operation the object is to obtain hardness, consistency, and complete neutrality of the soap. We begin to boil the paste gently with tolerably strong lyes. Some manufacturers proportion the quantity of lye to be used, and having put in the first, boil for eight hours or so, then draw off the lye, put in the second, boil again, draw off, and so on. Should the soap, during the intervals, become too liquid, which may happen if a too weak lye has been applied, some handfuls of salt must be added, or the soap boiled with a weak lye containing salt.

It may here be expedient to remark that, after each addition of lye, there should be, in taking up a portion by the spatula, some difficulty in running off the lye. Should this not be the case, water must be added, whereupon a quicker union of the alkali with the fat will be obtained.

The process is terminated when large, regular, and dry scales appear on the surface, and when these give elastic, brilliant, white scales, and are easily pulverized by rubbing them in the palms of the hands. The soap should then be covered, left for some time, and eventually removed in the ladles.

We have finally to mention that it is not at all necessary that the spent lye be of an alkaline test, as many manufacturers imagine. As soaps must be neutral combinations, this cannot be the case when the brines contain free alkali, for a portion of the latter will pass over in the soap, and in washing it will first dissolve, thus attacking hands and fabrics.

We deem it expedient to add here some remarks on

Marbling,

by which process the formation of veins in the soap is produced, either as the effect of the lye itself, or by the addition of foreign substances to the soapy paste. In order accurately to understand how marbling, in the first instance, may be obtained, we must remember that some kinds of sodas employed in the manufacture of soaps contain both the sulphuret of iron and sodium. In saponification a chemical combination takes place between these and the fatty acids, not yet satisfactorily demonstrated, though it is indisputable that such combinations are formed with iron for their base. These diffuse themselves throughout the mass, together with black sulphuret of iron (which is nothing else than what is called "*nigre*"), and being held in intimate suspension form bluish veins in the white ground, thus giving to the soap the appearance of marble. In newly cut castile soap these in course of time, after exposure to the atmosphere, assume a brownish color, a change caused by oxidation, the protosalt of iron being converted into persalt. If, however, the soda employed does not contain those constituents in itself, sulphate of protoxide of iron, or copperas, previously dissolved, is introduced into the soapy paste, say four ounces of the dry substance to 100 pounds of fat. By the chemical union of this oxide with the sulphuret of sodium, always existing in the crude soda, the coloring principle in the marbling of the soap is produced.

Mottled soap, made as above, is the *castile* soap of commerce; it contains necessarily less water than any other soap, and may hence be denominated *not fraudulent*, as a superabundance of water would, in any case, have precipitated the coloring matter, and consequently rendered veining impossible. For the successful and satisfactory operation of marbling, a thorough practical knowledge, the result of perseverance and experience, is absolutely requisite, for even the most enlightened theorist is often unable to teach the art. The essential point to observe, is to run the soap into the frames as soon as it presents the indications which experience has proved actually necessary for obtaining a good marbling. The eye, possibly, is the best guide in this respect, inasmuch as there are no fixed and precise regulations for the performance of this operation. The interspersion of the blue with the red veins (called *Manteau Isabelle* by the French), is effected by stirring some pulverized colcothar into the soap, after marbling in the ordinary way.

CHAPTER II.

NEW METHODS.

THE PROCESS OF MEGE MOURIES.

MEGE MOURIES, a distinguished French chemist, has recently found that the neutral fats in the oil seeds during germination, as well as in the animal organism during life, take the state of very movable globules, which offer to the action of reagents a great surface. In this globular state, fats show very particular properties, from which we will only mention those calculated to interest the reader of this book.

1. In the ordinary state, fat, as, for instance, tallow, soon becomes rancid upon exposure to air; in the globular state, in a milky form, however, or in the dry state, in the form of a white powder, it will remain unaltered for any length of time. For practical purposes, it is easily obtainable by mixing melted tallow of 113° F. with water of the same temperature, holding in solution five to ten per cent. of soap.

2. In the ordinary state, it is difficult to combine tallow as well as the other fatty bodies with hot salty caustic lyes, but in the globular state they absorb this lye immediately, in a proportion varying with the temperature. Each globule, as it is attacked from all sides by the alkali, gives in such a case its glycerine quickly off, and in such a degree that in a very

short time, each globule is transformed into a globule of a perfect soap filled with lye. Two or three hours are sufficient for obtaining such a result.

3. These saponified fat globules have the property, when heated over 140° F., of running off the surplus lye with which they are swelled or filled, and of retaining only water sufficient for ordinary soap. They thus eventually become transparent, and by stirring form a layer of melted soap over the lye containing the glycerine.

4. The saponification of this mass is so complete, that, for the preparation of stearic acid, it is only necessary to add a corresponding quantity of diluted sulphuric acid, whereupon sulphate of soda will be formed and the fatty acids separated. It is then only necessary to melt them by the introduction of steam, for the purpose of separating them from the solution of sulphate of soda, to let them crystallize, and press them cold. Stearic acid will be obtained unchanged, inodorous, and with a melting-point of 136 to 138° F., while the oleic acid, flowing off, will be nearly colorless.

The latter is even of a better quality than fixed oils, more desirable and useful for the manufacture of white soap of first quality, either alone or with other fatty substances. By using oleic acid alone (the glycerine being separated), it is only required to neutralize it with weak lye; the formation of soap then takes place immediately, which can be melted at once. If, however, the oleic acid be mixed with ordinary fats, the process described under 1. must be followed. Saponification can be effected in six hours, and in the course of twenty-four hours a soap can be prepared as neutral and good, and of the same detersive qualities, as the best old olive-oil soap, found in commerce. By this method, not only is more time saved, but no fat is lost in saponification, whereas in the ordinary process of boiling soap, no small quantity of fat is wasted, by running in the under lye.

Mège Mouriès manufactures at present in his factory near Paris 3000 lbs. of fatty acids daily, separating the whole amount of the stearic acid existing in the fats, and using, at the same time, the oleic acid obtained thereby for the manufacture of soap.

Fr. Knapp, who has repeated the experiments of Mège Mouriès, and found them correct, attributes the great efficacy of the globular state not so much to the globe form as to the microscopical smallness of the tallow globules, in which they can be attacked to their centres by the lye, while a larger lump of tallow, under the same circumstances, would soon be coated with a strata of soap, of a thickness which would render it impossible for the lye to penetrate. As to the saponification in the soapmaker's kettle, there is, strictly speaking, only an emulsion of fat obtained,—a homogeneous milky mass, formed by the union of the melted tallow with the lye; moreover, soap is partly, we might say simultaneously, produced with the first contact of these substances. This emulsion, after standing some hours in the cold, becomes gradually saponified. It might, however, be expected that the process of saponification would mature more rapidly under the influence of heat and agitation; but such is not the case, and the hypothesis given is, that in the boiling each fat globule is immediately enveloped in a layer of stearate of soda, which protects the nucleus from further saponification, just as drops of water thrown upon a hot iron at once acquire the spherical form, and continue rolling over it for a considerable time before they are fully converted into steam, which conversion, however, would have been more rapid at a lower temperature. In like manner, and upon the same principle, heated soap-bubbles are only denuded of their gelatinous coating, and the mass becomes a thickish soap solution rather than a chemical compound.

Again, concentrated soap in the heated mass will retain a considerable quantity of fat in solution, thereby diminishing the action of the alkali. This, indeed, may be remedied by the addition of a middling strong lye; but in any case refrigeration and quiet are found to promote the combination of fats with alkalies, after having been heated for a sufficient length of time to effect as minute a division of the molecules as possible with the characteristic form of an emulsion. For this purpose a temperature greater than 120° F. is not required.

Perutz, in his book, "Die Industrie der Fette und Oele,"* affirms that the facts discovered by Mège Mouriès, though no one has attempted to explain them, have, nevertheless, been successfully applied in soapmaking. To every rational manufacturer, he says, it must be known that saponification is produced with greater ease when the fat to be saponified is stirred for about an hour under a slight heat, about 140° F., with the so-called combination lye (*Verbindungs lauge*), and suffered to remain undisturbed for

---

* Berlin, 1866; J. Springer.

a night. As this mixture never reaches the boiling-point, it follows, for reasons already stated, that the globular emulsive state must be produced and saponification expedited.

With the view of improving Mège Mouriès' discovery, and for shortening the time consumed in boiling, Perutz proposes to add to the fat the whole quantity of lye necessary for saponification, and then proceed according to Mège Mouriès' plan, leaving the mixture quiet during the night. Up to the present day, however, soapmakers have not, in the beginning, added the entire quantity of lye required, because experience has shown that saponification is thereby rendered more difficult; but on the other hand, it has also been ascertained that saponification was more rapidly effected at a low temperature.

Pelouze's Process.

Pelouze, another French chemist, did not practically succeed so well as the former with his method of saponification by means of *sulphide of sodium.* His process, however, is of sufficient note and interest to demand a few remarks concerning it. When crystallized sulphuret of sodium is brought together with neutral fats, they are saponified at ordinary temperature and in a very short time. According to the inventor, a mixture of equal parts of crystallized sulphide of sodium, olive oil, and water, produces after ten, sometimes after five or six days, a thoroughly saponified paste, consisting of soap, glycerine, sulphhydrate of sodium, and the surplus of monosulphuret of sodium. When subjected to heat, however, sulphuretted hydrogen will escape, and soap remain. In this case, one equivalent of sulphide of sodium produces the same quantity of soap as one equivalent of pure caustic soda, but it is not at all necessary to make use of crystallized and chemically pure sulphide of sodium, for as much as that which is obtained by decomposing the sulphate of soda by charcoal can as well be employed. It is, moreover, much cheaper than the caustic soda. One important suggestion has been urged against Pelouze's process, and it is this: that the escape of sulphuretted hydrogen would be of very unhealthy influence on the workmen; but we have, on the other hand, reason to believe that Mr. Pelouze would not allow this gas to escape into the air, but collect it and make use of the sulphur therein contained in some way or other.

With regard to the appearance of the soap made in this way, it is asserted that it is exactly the same as that made in the ordinary way; but it is also said that it retains a disagreeable smell not easily destroyed. For ordinary purposes, however, such as scouring woollen fabrics, &c., this kind of soap may be well used.

In closing these remarks, we will mention that ten years ago, Prof. Wagner, of Würtzburg (Bavaria), affirmed that soaps may be made by means of the sulphides of calcium and barium.

Saponification by Pressure

has been patented in England by Messrs. Hodgson & Holden, and also by Mr. Davis. For this process the former parties employ a rotary, and the latter a perpendicular immovable cylinder, both of which are furnished with a man-hole door, a safety valve, feed and discharge pipes, and the ordinary appendages to such an apparatus. In both instances, also, steam is employed, and saponification effected at a high temperature. It is only recently that an American inventor, G. W. Rogers, Esq., of Lancaster, N. Y., has conceived the idea of conducting this operation at a *low* temperature. The advantages thus obtained are said to be considerable, among which may be mentioned *the saving of time*, twenty-five minutes, in some instances fifteen minutes, instead of one hour (requisite at a high temperature), being sufficient to produce a thorough saponification. Unlike the other contrivances, by this a *bleaching*, moreover, is effected, in consequence of which inferior qualities of stock can be employed. For mixing the materials, also, a tank heated by steam is simply used, and the mass thus prepared run into a cylinder (of boiler-iron, five-sixteenths of an inch thick) capable of holding one or more tons, and subjected to a pressure of about 400 pounds to a square inch by means of a force-pump, driven likewise by steam. In this cylinder the mass remains until complete saponification is effected, when it is drawn into the cooling frames and manipulated in the usual manner. Any of the ordinary mixtures for making soap are suitable, whilst the product is much firmer and more translucent.

In Mr. Rogers's process, moreover, no caustic soda is introduced, as the carbonate, even in relatively smaller quantities, answers every purpose.

Hawes, in London, produces

Saponification by Agitation.

Twenty gallons of lye, of 1.125 specific gravity, are employed for every 100 lbs. of tallow. The apparatus consists of a cylinder six feet in diameter and twelve feet in length, and is capable of working two and a half tons of tallow. Through the cylinder, lengthwise, a shaft extends, provided with radiating arms, to which an oscillating or rotary motion is communicated. Convenient doors are attached for charging and emptying the cylinder. After charging the container, agitation is commenced and continued for about three hours, when the whole is left undisturbed for awhile, and ultimately removed into an open boiler, and completed in the ordinary way.

CHAPTER III.

COMMON OR HOUSEHOLD SOAPS.

Hard Soaps.

Hard soaps are, as we have already mentioned, always soda soaps. There are boiled soaps in the trade as well as soaps made in the cold way, which latter method will be noticed in the next chapter. We can technically distinguish among the hard soaps thus, *grained soaps*, *i. e.*, those in which a separation of the under-lye has been made as described in Chapter I, Part II, and *filled soaps*, *i. e.*, those in which the whole contents of the boiling-pan are kept together and sold as soap. The cocoanut oil especially, is employed for the manufacture of filled soaps, because it is easily soluble in brine, requiring a very large quantity to separate them, and then they become so hard that they can scarcely be cut with a knife. The more solid constituents a fat contains, the harder the soap produced; the more oleine, however, the softer the soap. In mixing the fats in different proportions, we are therefore enabled to produce soaps of any consistency. But this also depends upon the strength of the lye used in the process. Weak and middling strong lyes will produce a light soap, while lyes of 25 to 30° B. will produce a soap heavier than water. Sometimes a small admixture of sulphate of soda is employed in making soap, for the special purpose of preventing too great solubility of it when used in washing. A soap not containing more than one per cent. of this substance, as, for instance, is the case with Dobbin's Electric Soap, is very well adapted for washing.

In the manufacture of soaps, one-third or one-fourth of fat is frequently substituted by rosin. Such soaps are called rosin soaps, but incorrectly denominated Yankee soaps, inasmuch as they have been first made in England. For the transformation of one hundred pounds of fat into soap, there are generally necessary twelve and a half pounds of solid caustic soda. It is however obvious, that this quantity must be more or less in proportion to the nature of the fat. We will, upon this basis, presently show how to calculate the quantity of lye of a certain degree, necessary for transforming a certain weight of fat into soap. Suppose we wish to saponify 400 lbs. of fat, how much lye of 12° Baumé will be requisite? A glance on the table, page 54, shows us that this lye is of a specific gravity of 1.08; 1 gallon of it weighs therefore $1.08 \times 8.3 =$ 8.9 lbs. (1 gallon of water has the weight of $8\frac{3}{10}$ lbs.), or the weight of 10 gallons of lye of 12° B. = 89 lbs. These contain 7.69 per cent. of caustic soda; 10 gallons will contain 6.84 lbs. of caustic soda. Now 6.84 lbs. is $\frac{1}{7}$th of the quantity for transforming 400 lbs. of fat into soap; hence $7 \times 10 = 70$ gallons must be employed, provided the lye be perfectly caustic and free of foreign salts.

We now pass over to a short description of the processes for manufacturing the different kinds of soap.

1. Tallow Soaps.

These are the most important, owing to the cheapness of the fat employed, and their introduction almost everywhere. But as so many methods for making this kind of soap exist, sufficient of themselves to fill a moderate-sized book, we will confine ourselves to a description of a process generally adopted in France, the country unrivalled for the cheapness and goodness of soaps.

Suppose we wish to saponify 1000 lbs. of fat. We commence by putting the tallow into the boiler, and melt it over a slow heat. This done, we add 70 to 80 gallons of lye of 10 to 12° B., stir well and keep a gentle fire for several hours. Should part of the fat separate from the mass, which is often the case, an oily liquid will be observed floating on the top. We must then add, gradually, 35 to 40 gallons of lye of 15 to 18° B. By this addition, the whole contents will soon form a homogeneous mass of a grayish-white color. In order to establish the necessary consistency to the paste, we must keep gentle boiling for several hours, adding every hour 6 to 7 gallons of lye of 20° B.

The time necessary for the first operation is from ten to twelve hours for 1000 lbs. of fat. After this we pass to the cutting process, and operate exactly as described above. It is absolutely essential that care be taken to stir the ingredients well while adding the salt. When the separation has taken place, we should leave it altogether quiet for several hours, and then draw off the colored under-lye; 90 gallons of lye of 25° should then be added; and we may also increase the heat, there being strong lye at the bottom of the pan which preserves the soap from burning. We then boil this mass from ten to twelve hours, adding every hour 5 gallons of lye of 25°. Four or five hours' boiling, however, will often be sufficient to saturate the soap, as described in Chapter I. This being accomplished, we should extinguish the fire, leave it quiet for an hour, and then draw off the under-lye. (It will measure from 25 to 30° B.) To complete the process, we must add about 50 gallons of lye of 4° B. This is suffered to boil gently for one and a half to two hours, stirring from time to time with the crutch, and finally extinguishing the fire and covering the pan. The soap will thus separate from the lye, and rise to the top. After five to six hours, while yet in a liquid state, we should pour it in the frames, taking due care that no lye be mixed with it. In the frames, it should be well crutched and stirred for some time. For neutralizing the disagreeable tallow odor, 1 to 2 ounces of a well-scented essential oil should be added to 100 lbs. of the soap, and after seven to eight days it may be cut. 100 lbs. of tallow will yield 165 to 170 lbs. of soap.

2. Tallow Rosin Soaps.

Rosin, when incorporated with a soap, to a certain amount, will make it more soluble and detersive. The lighter the rosin, the more it is valued; 15 per cent. of rosin with 85 per cent. of tallow answers a good purpose, but beyond that limit the soap is depreciated in color, in firmness, and quality. Even for the cheapest grade, the quantity of rosin should not exceed 33 per cent., for otherwise the soap will be clammy, soft, and unprofitable to the consumer. The rosin like fats can be saponified with alkali; 12 gallons of lye of 30° B. are needed for every 100 lbs. of rosin. Some soapmakers melt it with the fat in the commencement of the boiling for soap, but this method is not recommendable, as experience has proved that a much better product is obtained by first producing a tallow soap, and afterwards mixing the rosin soap with it, made in the meantime in a special kettle. Both mixtures (soaps) have to be stirred and beaten thoroughly for half an hour, and the whole passed through a sieve before they are filled into the frames, and therein well stirred and crutched. Some palm oil, when saponified with the tallow, will very much improve the appearance of the soap.

We will here briefly describe the preparation of

The Rosin Soap.

If 80 gallons of lye be put into a kettle of sufficient capacity, we should first boil the contents and then throw rosin in at intervals of five or six minutes, and in portions of 15 to 20 pounds, until 1320 pounds have been added. The rosin must be previously well pulverized, and while one workman is occupied with throwing it in, another should be constantly engaged in stirring it, as the mixture easily ascends. The heat must not be too rapidly increased, nor is it necessary that it should boil all the time, but simply keep the temperature near the boiling-point. It is, however, absolutely requisite to keep stirring the paste all the time, otherwise agglomerations of rosin will be formed. Saponification will be finished in two hours, and then the mixture, with the fat, is converted into soap as above described.

3. Cocoanut Oil Soap.

The cocoanut oil, as often mentioned, acts differently from any other fats, in combination with which weak lyes produce a milky mixture. Such lyes, however, have no effect upon cocoanut oil, for it can be seen floating on the top, whilst strong lyes of 25 to 30° very soon produce saponification throughout the whole mass.

Soapmakers generally use a lye of 27°, cold weighed, which will saponify an equal weight of cocoanut oil, 100 pounds, for instance, making nearly 200 pounds of soap. The process is very simple. The oil is put in the pan together with the lye, and then heat is applied. After continually stirring it for one or two hours, the paste will be seen gradually thickening, when the temperature of the heat applied should be moderated, but the stirring continued. After awhile the paste becomes transformed into a white semi-solid mass, which forms the soap, and this has to be filled immediately into the frames, because solidification takes place very quickly.

Often a mixture is used of equal parts of tallow and cocoanut oil, or of bleached palm oil and cocoanut oil, which yields a very fine soap. 90 to 95 per cent. of cocoanut oil, with 5 to 10 per cent. of natural palm oil, yields, also, a nice soap; and all these fats, when mixed with cocoanut oil in not too large proportions, will be as easily saponified as if the latter alone were used. Soapmakers, we may here remark, seldom, if ever, attempt to separate cocoanut oil with brine.

4. Palm Oil Soaps.

Palm oil is rarely used exclusively as a soap stock, but generally employed with an admixture of rosin, and it then yields the yellow soap; for white soap, however, these are employed in the bleached state. For some kinds of soap, palm oil is saponified with 5 to 10 per cent. of cocoanut oil; more is ofted used of the latter, and then filled soaps are obtained. Demi-palm is a soap consisting of equal parts of tallow and palm butter, to which is added a very small quantity of rosin and cocoanut butter.

The following are receipts for mixtures:

Palm oil,	300 lbs.
Tallow,	200 "
Rosin,	20 "
Tallow,	500 "
Palm oil,	300 "
Rosin,	200 "
Palm oil,	450 "
Cocoanut oil,	50 "
Hog fat,	550 "
Palm oil,	150 "
Cocoanut oil,	50 "
Clarified rosin,	50 "

Palm oil may be made into soap exactly in the same

way as tallow. If rosin be incorporated, it is better to produce first the combination of the rosin with the lye, and mix the same with the finished palm oil soap.

The soap made of the bleached palm oil is of a perfect whiteness, and as far as coloring is concerned can scarcely be distinguished from tallow. Palm soap becomes bleached when exposed to the light.

5. Different Soaps.

Such are the *red oil soap*, the *elaidin*, and the *silicated.* Red oil is not generally saponified by itself, but becomes so when combined with tallow or hog's fat. 600 lbs. of red oil and 400 lbs. of an animal fat, together with strong lye, say of 25 to 28° B., make a good soap. Red oil is easier made into soap than elaidin, which is the product of the action of nitrous acid upon oleic acid. Elaidin is like tallow, solid and hard, and gives a soap superior to the best tallow soap. It can be made into grain as well as into filled soap, and we may mention here that the union of the red oil or oleic acid with alkalies or the combination of its derivate, the elaidic acid, with alkali, or union of the rosin with soda or potash, is not a saponification, properly speaking, because chemically there is no formation of glycerine, but we may, nevertheless, use this term for expressing the process of combination.

Silicated soaps are seldom met with in trade, owing, in a great measure, to the fact that the method of preparing them requires large percentages of soluble glass, and another, according to Mr. Dieterichs, chemist of the Atlantic Quartz Company, in West Philadelphia, because their preparation was not understood. This gentleman has correctly stated that the fat soap in which the soluble glass is stirred must be of a perfect neutrality, for if there be the least trace of a fatty acid, silica will be precipitated and afterwards soda will effloresce. Not more than 20 per cent. of soluble glass (marking 35° B.) should ever be taken.*

Soft Soaps.

The difference between soda and potash soaps consists in this,—the first are hard, but the latter are soft. The former can therefore be purified by several operations, and brought to a water amount of a certain limit, while the latter keep the smeary form, and are brought in commerce with all their impurities, and the whole amount of water they can hold. If it be asked what advantage a soft or potash soap offers, we are told that it is easier soluble than soda soap, and also cheaper. With the first point we must agree, though it is easy enough to make a solution of soda soap, provided we heat it, but not so with the latter. It is certainly not cheaper than soda soap, as we will show hereafter.

The equivalent of caustic soda is 40, that of the potassa 56; *i. e.*, we must have 40 parts of soda for transforming a certain quantity of fat into soap, while we need 56 parts of potassa for doing the same. Now as the price of the potash is at least twice as much as

---

* Soluble glass, well adapted for the special purpose of making soap, is sold by Feuchtwanger, manufacturing chemist, Cedar Street, New York.

that of the caustic soda, it follows that we spend about three and a half times as much by employing potassa as we would do by using soda.

It is true that if fish oil is employed for making soft soaps, we get a cheap article; but can we not as well saponify the same raw materials with soda?

For the manufacture of soft soaps, hempseed oil, linseed oil, poppy oil, rapeseed, colza, whale, and seal oils are used.

Saponification is commenced with a lye of 9 to 11° B., and the contents of the kettle kept boiling until the paste becomes of sufficient consistency to draw threads, as it were, out of a streaky substance. It then undergoes the process of clear-boiling, for which purpose a lye of 25° B. should be used. Stirring must be done all the time, but when the paste does not sink any more (first it ascends), boils quietly, and shows the formation of scales, it may be considered complete. The barrels should be immediately filled, in which it is to be offered to the trade. The quality of the soft soaps is estimated according to their consistency. Consistent soaps are preferable to inconsistent ones. *Green soap* was formerly made of hempseed oil. It is now, however, made principally of whale oils, but as they have a yellow color, and consumers are accustomed to the green color of the hempseed oil soap, manufacturers mix the soaps made of the whale oils, with finely powdered indigo, or the indigo-sulphate of lime, which is prepared by dissolving indigo in sulphuric acid, diluting it with water, and saturating the whole with lime-milk.

The black soft soap is made by adding to the soap

a mixture of a solution of copperas and logwood or gall-nuts.

As a glance at our table in Chapter V, Part II, will show at once the composition of different smear soaps, we therefore conclude this chapter, and in our next call attention to a much more important branch of soapmaking,—we mean the manufacture of fancy or toilet soaps.

CHAPTER IV.

THE MANUFACTURE OF TOILET SOAPS.

In the manufacture of toilet or fancy soaps, exactly the same crude materials are employed as for the common or household soaps, but they are in a more refined or pure state, and the superior fats, as hog's fat, cocoanut oil, and olive oil, are substituted for the inferior. The soaps obtained by those materials are also generally colored and well scented by the odorous principles of plants.

All the fine English soaps are chiefly made by boiling, but as this process has already been described, we shall confine our remarks to the respective receipts for the different kinds found in the trade.

Most of the fancy soaps in this country, are, however, little pan soaps, *i. e.*, soaps made in the cold way, which process we will describe hereafter.

We shall, moreover, mention something on the coloring and perfuming of soaps, and then give receipts for most of the different kinds of soaps.

Process of Making Soaps in the Cold Way.

First the fat is melted in a well-cleaned iron or copper kettle, at a low temperature; then it is filtered through fine linen or muslin into another kettle.* To the fat, which, however, must not be warmer than 104° F., the lye is gradually added. In the soaps made after the cold way, a very strong lye is used, generally one of 36° B., and for a certain quantity of fat just half of it employed; say, for 80 lbs. of fat, 40 lbs. of lye (less when the lye is stronger).

The lye must be entirely clear and colorless, but it is not necessary that it be heated previously, when it has been kept in a warm room. For stirring it, a broad paddle of boxwood must be used, having sharp edges at its lower end, rounded at its upper end, so that it may be the more easily handled.

The paddling should be continued until a ring drawn with the spatula may be recognized. At this immediate juncture, the necessary coloring matter and perfumery should be added. The paste should then be run into frames previously lined with linen, so carefully that no folds be formed in the edges of the box.

Each frame should be entirely filled with the mass, and well closed with the margin of the linen and a wooden cover, and the whole left for twelve hours, by which time saponification will have been produced, when it will be seen that the mass, which was nearly

* Often the fat has to be further purified. This is done by boiling it with one-third of water for about ten minutes, and straining it off. Some add for 100 lbs. of fat, 6 ounces of salt, 3 ounces of fine pulverized alum. They then let it remain quiet for some hours until it becomes what is called "figging." Mr. August Bermon, in Nizza, purifies the fats which he uses for the absorption of certain flower odors in a particular manner. After having it boiled with a solution of salt in the above proportions, and thus clarified, he adds 4 ounces of benzone to 100 lbs. of fat and 1 gallon of rose-water, and skims it under a gentle boiling. The fat thus purified can be kept for years without getting rancid.

cold when run into the frames, has undergone a spontaneous reaction, raising the temperature sometimes over 175° F. Under the influence of this temperature the different constituent principles of the materials are combined, and a soap produced of a quality almost resembling that of the boiled soaps.

At the expiration of the twelve hours stated above, the soap may be taken out of the frame, cut and dried. Some add about one-tenth of potassa lye to the soda lye, for the purpose of increasing the solubility, and consequently the quality of the soap; for when no potassa is added these soaps are generally hard. Of such kind of soaps, 100 lbs. of fat will yield about 150 lbs.

KURTEN'S TABLE,

Showing the composition and yield of Soap by the Cold Process, from Concentrated Lye, and mixtures of Cocoa Oil with Palm Oil, Lard, and Tallow.

Kinds of Soap.	Tallow.	Cocoanut Oil.	Palm Oil.	Lard.	Lye.	Degrees.	Salt Water.	Degrees.	Potash.	Degrees.	Product.
Cocoanut Oil, No. 1, ...	..	100	..	..	56	36	..	..	..	..	153
Paris Toilette (round), . .	20	30	..	8	31	36	..	..	5	36	87
" " " . .	..	25	..	75	50–52	36	..	..	..	..	150
Windsor (square), ...	66	34	..	..	77	30	..	..	13	30	185
Shaving, No. 1, ...	66	34	..	..	...	..	..	..	..	..	..
	or		..	..	120	27	..	..	..	..	214
	33	34	33	..	...	..	..	..	..	..	..
Shaving, No. 2, ...	33	34	33	..	120	27	12	12	..	..	226
Washing, No. 1, ...	60	40	..	..	...	..	..	..	..	..	..
	or		..	..	125	27	25	12	..	..	244
	30	40	30	..	...	..	..	..	..	..	..
Washing, No. 2, ...	40	60	..	..	...	..	..	..	..	..	..
	or		..	..	135	27	50	15	..	..	278
	..	60	40	..	...	..	..	..	..	..	..
Ordinary Cocoanut Oil, . .	..	100	..	..	...	..	..	..	..	..	..
	or										
	10	90	..	..	225	21	75	12	..	..	400
	or										
	..	90	10	..	...	..	..	..	..	..	..

TRANSPARENT SOAPS

are prepared by dissolving well-dried soaps in alcohol; but we must remember that all kinds of soaps cannot, with equal facility, be thus transformed. It is difficult, for instance, to work up into a solid consistency soaps made of olive oil, when treated with alcohol, and they invariably assume the opaque form. A good suet soap should always be preferred, and rosin tallow soaps yield readily yellow soaps of a remarkable transparency.

The first step necessary for making these kinds of soaps, is to cut them into very thin ribbons, which can be done with a knife, or better still, with a soap-mill, as represented in Fig. 7, page 108. The soap having been thus cut, is next extended on strong paper, and exposed to the air and sun until it is thoroughly dried. It is then pulverized in a marble mortar, and passed through a fine sieve. The powder thus obtained is directly dissolved in strong boiling alcohol. While the soap is liquid, the colors and perfumes are incorporated with it.

Three and a half gallons of alcohol of the specific gravity of 0.849 are generally apportioned for 50 lbs. of soap. A still, heated by steam or hot water, is for the most part used for this operation, as a considerable quantity of alcohol would be lost in a common heating-pan, and the direct application of fire would destroy the beauty and transparency of the resulting product.

Fig. 6 represents an apparatus suitable for manufacturing transparent soaps on a large scale. A is a water-bath mounted on a furnace of ordinary construction, and having a smoke-stack M. Instead of a water-bath, if a steam boiler be at hand, the tank A can be mounted on a wooden framework, the furnace dispensed with, and steam supplied through the pipe G. B is the soap vessel; it is best made of copper, and in it the stirring apparatus D D D D is mounted,

Fig. 6.

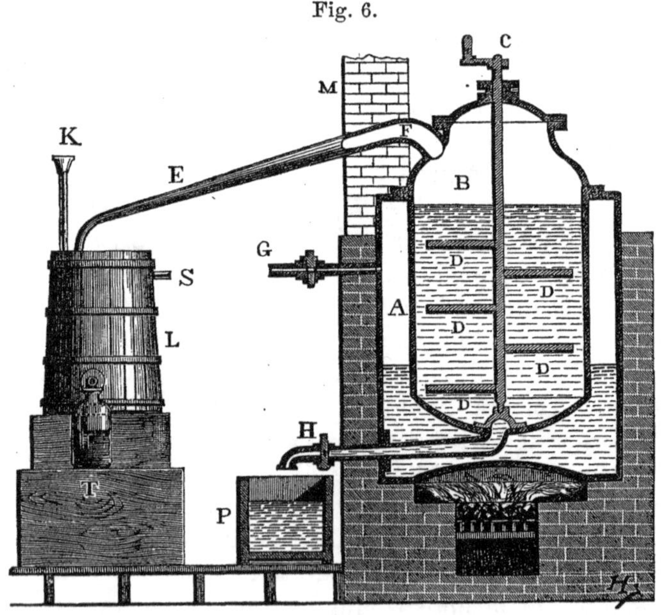

moved by the crank C, or other gearings. The vessel B can be opened at the top for the purpose of cleaning it, and it has also at the bottom a draw-off cock H, to run off the charge into the mould-frame P. F is a pipe leading from the vessel B to a worm in the tank L. K and S are the water inlet and outlet of the cooling tank L. T is the bottle in which the surplus of alcohol is received.

The following is the *modus operandi* of making transparent soap: Soap and alcohol are introduced into the vessel B, and heat applied; by the latter, the water in the bath will enter into ebullition and transfer its heat to B, the contents of which will also enter into boiling, when by the action of the alcohol the soap will be dissolved. To facilitate this dissolving process, a rotating movement is given to the agitateur. During this part of the operation, a portion of the alcohol is volatilized and condensed in the serpentine, lying in the cooling barrel L. About five pints of the three and a half gallons of the alcohol, already mentioned, must be distilled off, and then we may be sure that the liquefaction is complete, and the fluid soap of the right consistency. This accomplished, the heat is stopped, and the mass left undisturbed for a few minutes, in order that all foreign materials may settle. The liquid is finally turned into the moulds duly arranged for them, the capacity of which should be one-third larger than the size of the forms intended, thus allowing for the shrinking of the soap material. A light strata of dust adhering, the soap, when dry (a process of several days), sometimes assumes a dull appearance. This, however, is easily removed, and a brilliant neat surface rendered by rubbing it with fine linen saturated in alcohol.

Coloring Soaps.

For the coloring of the ordinary fancy soaps, mineral colors are employed; but for the superior toilet and the transparent soaps, organic pigments are used, necessarily and materially enhancing the price of them.

Generally speaking, the *red* coloring matter is derived from vermilion or chrome red, the *violet* from fuchsine solved in glycerine, the *red-brown* and *brown* from caramel and the various kinds of umber. For *green*, the veritable chrome green is taken; a beautiful (vegetable) green is obtained by stirring in the soap, saponified with 7 to 10 per cent. of palm oil, some smalts or ultramarine. For *blue*, smalts or ultramarine is taken. *Yellow* is obtained by mixing some per cent. of palm butter with the fat to be saponified. For *black*, common lampblack is used.

Fine toilet soaps, as well as transparent soaps, *i. e.*, soaps which have been taken up by rectified spirit, may be colored as follows:

A *red color* may be given with tincture of dragon's blood or liquid carmine. *Rose*, with tincture of carthamine or of archil. *Yellow* and *orange* with tincture of annotto or saffron. *Blue* and *violet* with tincture of litmus, or of alkanet-root, or with soluble Prussian blue (basic), or a very little pure indigo in impalpable powder. *Green*, by a mixture of blue and yellow.

Perfuming Soaps.

The process of perfuming is generally done when the paste is already in the frame, as, if added in the pan, when the soap is yet hot, most of the essential oils would be volatilized. It is best to mix the colors and the perfumes together with some alcohol or glycerine, and stir it well in the paste. The method of perfuming soaps in the cold state is extensively adopted in France. It produces very fine kinds of soaps, for if very highly perfumed soaps are to be prepared, and the perfumes are added to the melted material, even when in the frame, much of their value and odor are lost by volatilization.

The process is very simple, though much mechanical work is required; for, a very pure and clarified soap having been made from the best materials obtainable, it is then run into some kind of a circular planing machine, where it is cut in very thin shavings; these shavings are then mixed with the proportionate admixture of color and perfumes, and passed through a machine called *la broyeuse*, which, in large factories, is set in motion by steam. In this machine the scrapings are passed through cylinders with opposite motions of different velocity; but they must pass through it five or six times, or until they show a uniform appearance; they then form nice little scales.

Often both of these machines are combined together, as is the case in the following, from which a description has been kindly furnished to us by a practical French engineer. Finally the soap-scales are brought into a compact form by the "Peloteuse."

Description of the French Soap-mill and of the Shaping Machine, "Peloteuse."

Fig. 7 represents a front view of the mill used for dividing the soap in small shavings, and triturating it with colors, perfumes, &c., previous to its being formed by pressure into bars and tablets by the machine called "Peloteuse," represented by Fig. 8.

Fig. 7.

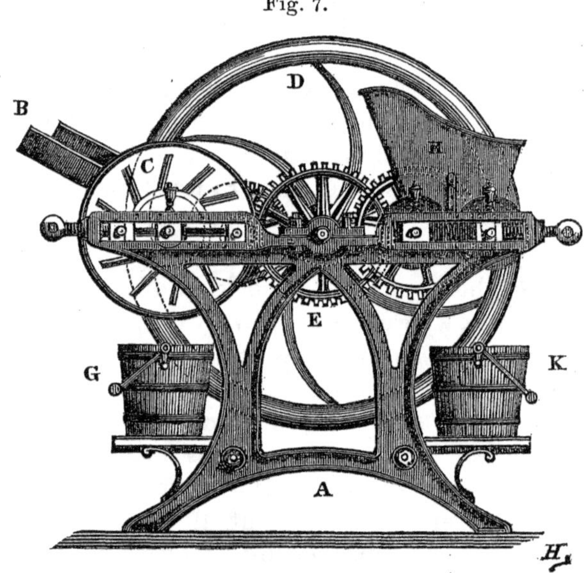

Fig. 7, representing the mill, is composed of two frames, A A, bolted together by suitable braces, on which the central shaft is mounted, bearing the fly-wheel D and gearings E, so arranged as to transmit movement to the right or left with corresponding different results. On one side the speed of the machinery is multiplied to set in rapid motion the shav-

Fig. 8.

ing disk C. This disk, provided with sharp cutters, is, in fact, a circular plane, upon which the bar of soap falls by its own gravity, and sliding on the inclined plane B, is cut into thin slices or shavings, which fall into the pail G placed underneath to receive them.

On the other side of the shaft and gearings E, the motion is communicated to a set of rolls, upon which the trough H is mounted. In this trough the sliced soap is placed, and there the proper perfumes and colors are added, and the action of the rolls is brought to bear upon the mass for the purpose of thoroughly mixing the different ingredients, and working them up, as it is termed, until they are fit for being shaped into bars and tablets. In this state the mass is dropped into the pail K previous to its final removal into the Peloteuse.

This machine, Fig. 8, is composed of a strong table C, supported on trestles D, D, D, upon which a powerful box-press, A, is mounted, built similarly to a sausage-stuffing machine. There is also a piston acted upon by the screw E, worked by gearings F and pulleys G. The box A of the press being filled with the prepared soap paste, the lid is let down upon it, and properly secured by the fastenings B. The press is now put in motion, and the soap paste is forced out at the end P by the holes left for that purpose, so that by varying the shape of said holes, the shape of the bars issuing therefrom will be different. These, on leaving the press-box A, rest on the endless belt K, upon which they are cut to the proper length, generally to be transferred to the screw stamping press, there to receive the finishing touch. The handle H puts the motion of the press entirely under the control of the operator, so that he can reverse the motion of the press by moving this lever.

FORMULÆ FOR SOAPS.

WINDSOR SOAP.

1. (White.) The best "English Windsor Soap" is made of a mixture of

Olive oil	1 part,
Ox suet, or tallow	8 or 9 parts,

saponified with a lye of caustic soda, and scented after removal from the boiler. The ordinary, in general, is merely curd-soap, scented, whilst semi-liquid, with oil of caraway, supported with a little oil of bergamot, lavender, or origanum. To the finer qualities a very little oil of cassia, or of almonds, or of the essences of musk and ambergris, is also commonly added. The usual proportion of the mixed oils for good qualities, is 1½ lbs. per cwt., and 2 lbs., at the least, for the finer ones, exclusive of the alcoholic essences, if any be employed.

The fatty basis of "French Windsor Soap" is usually *hog's lard*, with the addition of a little palm oil.

2. (Brown.) Originally this was the white variety that had become yellow and brown by age. It now merely differs from the preceding in being colored with a little caramel, or (less frequently), with umber or brown ochre.

HONEY SOAP—*Savon au miel.*

The ordinary "honey soap" is merely the finest bright-colored yellow (resin) soap, colored by the addition of a little palm oil or palm oil soap, and scented with oil of rose geranium, or oil of ginger-grass, supported or not with a little oil of bergamot or verbena. Some of the finer kinds are made of—

Olive oil soap Palm oil soap	} of each . . .	1 part.
White curd soap	. . . . .	3 parts,

deepened in color, whilst in the liquid state, with a little palm oil, or annotto (of its tincture), and scented with 1 to $1\frac{1}{2}$ ounces of essential oils per $\frac{1}{2}$ lb., or 1 to $1\frac{1}{2}$ lbs. per cwt.

Musk Soap—*Savon musqué.*

The basis is generally a good ox suet or tallow soap; the scent, essence of musk, or oil of musk, supported with a little of the oils of bergamot, cinnamon, and cloves. The quantity of the essence used depends on the intended quality (fragrance) of the product. The coloring matter is usually caramel. This soap, when sufficiently scented, imparts a faint but persistent odor to the skin, which is very agreeable. "Ambergris soap" is prepared in a similar way.

Glycerinated Soap.

Any mild toilet soap, with which about $\frac{1}{25}$th to $\frac{1}{20}$th of its weight of glycerine has been intimately incorporated whilst in the liquid state. It is generally tinged of a red or rose color, or orange-yellow. It is variously scented; but oil of bergamot, or rose geranium (ginger-grass), supported with a little oil of cassia, or cassia supported with essential oil of almonds, appear to be its favorite perfumes. We are obliged to Struve, proprietor of a large soap factory in Leipsic (Germany), for the following receipt for glycerinated soap:

40 lbs. of tallow, 40 lbs. of lard, and 20 lbs. of cochin cocoanut oil, are saponified with 45 lbs. of soda lye and 5 lbs. of potash lye of 40° Baumé, when the soap is to be made in the cold way. To the paste are then added—

Pure glycerine	6 lbs.
Oil of Portugal	½ ounce.
Oil of bergamot	⅓ ounce.
Bitter almond oil	5 ounces.
Oil of vitivert	3 ounces.

ALMOND SOAP—*Savon d'amande amère.*

The best quality is usually white curd soap, with or without the addition of $\frac{1}{9}$th to $\frac{1}{7}$th of its weight of olive oil soap, scented with essential oil of almonds in the proportion of about 1 ounce to each 4½ to 5 lbs., or 1½ lbs. to the cwt; very fine. The addition of a little oil of cassia (say 4 or 5 ounces per cwt), improves it. Second and inferior qualities are scented with nitrobenzole, the artificial oil of almonds, instead of the genuine or natural oil.

VIOLET SOAP—*Savon à la violette.*

1. Any white toilet soap strongly scented with essence of orris root, and colored, or not, with tincture of litmus, or a little levigated smalts, ultramarine, or indigo.

2.

White curd soap	3 lbs.,
Olive oil soap	1 lb.,
Palm oil soap	3 lbs.,

melted together, and further scented (best cold) with

a little essence of orris root, and colored, or not, at will. Very fragrant, but it does not take color very well.

BOUQUET SOAP—*Savon au bouquet.*

1. Take of—

White curd soap, finest	. . .	17½ lbs.,
Olive oil soap	. . . .	2½ lbs.,
Oil of bergamot	. . . .	1 ounce,
" cassia	of each . .	1½ drachms,
" cloves		
" sassafras		
" thyme		
" neroli	. . . . .	1 drachm,
ochre, brown, levigated	. .	2 ounces,

and proceed as for almond soap. Highly and agreeably fragrant. It may be varied by substituting *English oil of lavender* for the "neroli."

2.	White curd soap	. . . . .	20 lbs.
	Oil of bergamot	. . . . .	2⅝ ounces.
	" cloves	. . . . .	½ drachm.
	" neroli	. . . . .	½ drachm.
	" sassafras	. . . . .	⅓ drachm.
	" thyme	. . . . .	⅓ drachm.

Colored with 2½ ounces brown ochre.

ROSE SOAP.

1. Take of

Palm oil soap (in shavings) . .	3 lbs.
White curd soap (finest in shavings)	2 lbs.
Soft water	¼ pint.

Melt them together in a bright copper pan, set in a water-bath. Add of

Vermilion (levigated) . . .	¼ ounce.

and when the mixture has cooled a little, stir in of

Otto of roses (finest)	. . .	2 drachms.
Oil of bergamot	. . . .	1½ drachms.
" cinnamon } " cloves }	of each . .	¾ drachm.
" rose geranium	. . .	½ drachm.

Mix well, and pour the mass into an open-bottomed wooden frame, set on a polished marble slab.

Sometimes it is colored with tincture of dragon's blood, or of archil, instead of vermilion.

2.	White curd soap	. . . .	20 lbs.
	Esprit de rose .	. . . .	1⅓ ounces.
	Oil of cloves	. . . .	½ drachm.
	" cinnamon	. . . .	⅓ drachm.
	" bergamot	. . . .	1 drachm.
	" neroli .	. . . .	⅓ drachm.

Colored with 2 ounces vermilion.

Cinnamon Soap.

This is usually a mixture of tallow and oil soaps, like that of "*Savon au bouquet*," colored with about ¼ lb. of yellow ochre, and scented with 1 ounce of oil of cinnamon (supported with a little oil of bergamot and sassafras) to each 7 lbs.

The following is a very good formula for making it. Take of

White curd soap, (finest)	. .	6 lbs.
Palm oil soap	. . . .	3½ lbs.
Cocoanut oil soap .	. . . .	1 lb.
Oil of cinnamon	. . . .	1½ ounce.
" bergamot } " sassafras }	of each . .	¼ ounce.
Lavender (English)	. . .	1 drachm.
Yellow ochre (levigated)	. .	¼ lb.

Oil of cassia is commonly substituted for the oil of cinnamon, and always so in second and in inferior qualities.

LAVENDER SOAP.

The basis of the "Windsor soap," scented with English oil of lavender (1 to 1½ fluid ounces per 7 lbs.), supported with a little oil of bergamot and the essences of musk and ambergris. It is often colored with a little tincture of litmus, or the corresponding mineral pigments.

ORANGE FLOWER SOAP.

As "savon à la rose;" but using pure neroli, supported with a "dash" of the essences of ambergris and Portugal, instead of otto of roses, as scent. A delicate yellow tinge is sometimes given to it. The French soap, "à la fleur d'orange," is scented with equal parts of neroli and geranium.

RONDELETIA SOAP.

The basis of cinnamon, rose, or Windsor soap, scented with 1 to 1½ ounces of the mixed oils and essences used for "essence" or "esprit de rondeletia" to each 7 lbs. It is kept both white and slightly colored. The appropriate colors are those used for bouquet, cinnamon, honey, and brown Windsor soap. Sometimes it is tinged like rose soap.

FLOWERS OF ERIN.

White curd soap, scented with oil of roses .	1 drachm.
Esprit of violet	½ fluid ounce.
" jasmine	⅓ "
" patchouly	¼ "
" vanilla	¼ "

Tinged green or rose.

PRIMROSE SOAP—*Savon à la primevère.*

This has usually a similar basis to "honey soap," and is faintly scented with mixed oils similar to those used as "cowslip perfume," and colored of a pale yellow, or greenish-yellow.

CREAMS AND ESSENCES OF SOAP FOR SHAVING.

SHAVING PASTE.

White soft soap . . .	4 ounces.
Honey soap (finest) . . .	2 "
Olive oil	1 ounce.
Water	1 or 2 tablespoonfuls.
Carbonate of soda . . .	1 drachm.

Melt them together and form a paste, adding a little proof-spirit, and scent at will. Some melt with the soap about 1 drachm of spermaceti. Produces a good lather with either hot or cold water, which dries slowly on the face.

PEARL SOAP—*Cream Soap.*

Take white soft soap (lard potash soap), recent, but moderately firm, and beat it in small portions at a time, in a marble mortar, until it forms a white homogeneous mass, and "pearls," as it is technically called; essential oil of almonds, q. s., supported with a little oil of bergamot, or of cassia, being added during the pounding.

SHAVING ESSENCE OR FLUID.

1.	White hard soap (in shavings) . .	¼ lb.
	Rectified spirit	1 pint.
	Water	¼ pint.

Perfume at will.

Put them into a strong bottle of glass or tin, cork it close, set it in warm water for a short time, and occasionally agitate it briskly until solution be complete. After repose, pour off the clean portion from the dregs (if any) into clean bottles for use, and at once closely cork them. If the solution be not sufficiently transparent, a little rectified spirit should be added to it before decantation; a little spirit (fully proof) may be added if it be desired to render it thinner. If much essential oil be used to perfume it, the transparency of the product will be lessened.

2. Take of—

White soft soap	¼ lb.
Liquor of potassa . . .	2 fluid drachms.
Rectified spirit	1 pint.

Perfume at will.

Proceed as before. The product of both the above is excellent. Chiefly used for shaving by travellers and others, to avoid the trouble of carrying or keeping a soap-box. By simply rubbing two or three drops on the skin, and applying the shaving-brush, previously slightly dipped in water, a good lather is produced. The choice of perfume is a mere matter of taste, as with the toilet soaps. 15 to 20 drops of *essence of musk* or *ambergris*, 1 fluid drachm of any of the ordinary *fragrant essences* or *esprits*, or 12 or 15 drops of *essential oil* (simple or mixed), per pint, are sufficient for the purpose; a corresponding name being given to the preparation, as "Essence" or "Esprit de savon à la rose," "Essence royale pour la barbe."

CHAPTER V.

VALUEMETRY,

OR ESTIMATION OF SOAPS IN REGARD TO THEIR COMMERCIAL VALUE.

WE distinguish *soft soaps* (potash soaps) from *hard soaps* (soda soaps), and *filled soaps* from *grain soaps.* In regard to the organic ingredients, we may arrange them in two groups, *rosin soaps* and *fat* or *oil soaps.* Among the latter, we may mention as the more important, tallow soaps, palm oil, cocoanut oil, and olive oil soaps. In addition to these, however, there are many mixtures of fatty substances in combination with alkalies, known as soaps. In good soap there is a definite proportion between the water, the alkaline base, and the fatty acids. It must be neutral, *i. e.*, there should be no excess either of the base, or of the constituents of the fat, and at the same time it must be free from salt, or an excess of water, which is virtually as much of an adulteration as an admixture of salt, soda, alum, bone ashes, glauber salt, or other substances. A good soap is easily soluble in alcohol, leaving scarcely 1 per cent. of solid residue, and forms a gelatinous liquid in boiling water.*

* I once received a whitish-gray marbled soap for analysis, which showed the following properties: It was much softer than an ordinary curd soap, so that it could be cut like butter, and drops of water issued from each cutting. When I left it in a dry

It may here be mentioned, that a hard or marbled soap should not contain more than 25 per cent. of water, rosin soap not more than 40, and a soft soap not more than 52.

For cocoanut oil soaps, however, a larger amount of water than 52 per cent. may be allowed.

In the yellow soap, a part of the fat is justifiably replaced by 10 to 25 per cent. of rosin.

The proportions here named may be regarded as a standard, and whenever they are increased or replaced by a substitute, it may be said that they generally diminish the good quality of the soap. The introduction of a foreign substance may, in a few cases, be justifiable. Some believe that an excess of alkali is necessary, in order that the soap may be used in spring water without loss. It may be mentioned, that in this case, the salts of lime and magnesia contained in the water, form *insoluble* compounds with the fatty acids of the soap, and these are of no cleansing effect. But whenever spring water is used for washing, a small admixture of carbonate of soda is more advantageous than the appliance of a soap containing free alkalies.

For the better elucidation of the composition of the different kinds of soap, we give here the following table.

---

place, it did not only effloresce a good deal of soda, but also crystals of soda were formed in the interior, so that the soap cracked throughout. Heated on the water-bath, it soon became liquid, and left upon evaporation 22 per cent. of a solid residue, consisting of cocoanut oil soap and carbonate of soda.

HARD SOAPS.

NAME.	Fatty Acids.	Fat and Rosin.	Dry Soda.	Dry Potassa.	Salt. (Na. Cl.)	Lime and insoluble residue.	Water.	Name of the Analyst.
American Curd Soap	67.5	..	7.7	..	..	..	24.2	Morfit.
Holt's Yellow Soap	..	74.	7.08	..	..	..	18.92	Kent.
American Soap Company's Soap	..	35.	5.	..	..	40.	20.	"
Colgate's Yellow Soap	..	64.	7.29	..	..	..	28.71	"
" " "	..	56.2	9.	..	3.8		31.	Morfit.
" Nonpareil" Soap	..	36.2	5.2	..	5.25		51.9	"
Beatty's Soap (patent)	..	37.	5.5	..	0.5		52.	"
Butterfield's Soap	..	32.5*	9.2	..	1.7	2.	55.	"
German Curd Soap, prepared from potashes after having been kept several years	81.25	..	8.55	1.77	..	..	8.4	Heeren.
White Tallow Soap (Leipsic)	76.3	..	8.8		..	..	14.7	Abendroth.
" " "	50.	..	9·4		..	..	29.8	"
" " "	45.	..	9.8		..	..	38.	"
Marseilles Soap	67.16	..	7.82	..	1.08	..	23.94	Bolley.
" "	68.01	..	7.25	..	1.33	..	23.41	"
" "	66.99	..	7.8	..	4.	..	21.21	"
French White Soap	50.2	..	4.6	..	..	..	45.2	Thénard.
" Marbled Soap	64.	..	6.	..	..	..	30.	"
White London Toilet Soap	75.	..	9.	..	..	..	16.	Ure.

* 10.5 Rosin and 22 Fatty Acids.

HARD SOAPS—*Continued.*

NAME.	Fatty Acids.	Fat and Rosin.	Dry Soda.	Dry Potassa.	Salt. (Na. Cl.)	Lime and insoluble residue.	Water.	Name of the Analyst.
Poppy Oil Soap	76.	..	7.	..	..	..	17.	Ure.
Glasgow Brown Resin Soap	..	70.	6.5	..	..	..	23.5	"
Glasgow White Soap	60.	..	6.4	..	..	..	33.6	"
Manchester Palm Oil Soap	56.6	..	7.2	..	..	..	36.	O'Neill.
London Curd Soap	52.	..	6.	..	..	..	42.	Ure.
London Marine Soap	22.	..	4.5	..	..	..	73.5	"
SOFT SOAPS.								
French Fulling Soap	62.	..	..	11.5	..	..	26.5	Verviers.
Savon mou ordinaire	42.8	..	..	9.1	..	..	48.	Chevreul.
Savon vert	44.	..	..	9.5	..	..	46.5	Thénard.
Belgian Green Soap	36.	..	..	7.	..	..	57.	Ure.
Scotch Rape-Oil Soap	51.66	..	..	10.	..	..	38.33	"
Gallipoli Soft Soap	48.	..	..	10.	..	..	42.	"
London Soft Soap	45.	..	..	8.5	..	..	46.5	"
Manchester Soft Soap	42.	..	..	8.25	..	..	47.	O'Neill.
" "	37.5	..	..	8.81	..	..	44.	"
" "	36.75	..	..	9.57	..	..	47.75	"

We now pass on to the estimation of the soaps.

(*a.*) *Determination of the Amount of Water.*—To ascertain this, a small quantity should be taken from the inside as well as the outside, and finely scraped. A certain portion of it should then be weighed (say 80 grains), placed in a concentric ring of a water-bath, previously filled with a saturated solution of nitre, and heated to the boiling-point. The capsule, with the soap, should then be in the bath from two to three hours, during which time the solution of the nitre is kept boiling, and if too much water evaporate during the process, fresh should be added. We recommend this addition of a solution of nitre, instead of water alone, because the temperature of the boiling-point of the former is specially adapted for thoroughly expelling the water contained in the soap, which will not be the case if the temperature of the boiling water only be employed. A boiling solution of salt also will not give the necessary heat. When the capsule, with the soap, has been in the water-bath for several hours, it should be taken away and weighed, the weight noted, and the capsule replaced. If after one or two hours' additional heating, the weight is not diminished, it is evident that all the water is expelled.

Suppose now, the original weight of the soap taken for analysis were 80 grains, the weight after it was dried only 67 grains, then it follows that the soap contained

$$\frac{(80-67)\times 100}{80} = 16.25 \text{ per cent. of water.}$$

(*b*.) *Determination of the Amount of Fat.*—The amount of fat contained in a soap is found by decomposing the soap with an acid. 80 grains of the sample should then be taken from the inside as well as from the outside, where it is obviously drier. Put it in a porcelain dish, and add to it twenty or thirty times its weight of sulphuric acid, diluted twelve times, and heat the whole over a lamp, until the fat is floating on the top. For separating it, without loss, from the liquid contents of the dish, a quantity of white wax equal to that of the soap taken, should be added to the whole at the end of the operation, and suffered to melt with the fat, and thus a consistent solid and hard disk is then obtained, which can easily be separated by a spatula from the liquid contents of the dish. The fat cake should then be put on a filter, and washed with pure water until blue litmus paper does not become reddened. For drying, it should be kept in fusion in a porcelain capsule, until no decrepitation is produced; when it should be cooled and weighed. From the total weight, first the weight of the added wax is deduced, the remainder represents the fat contained in the soap (rosin soap excepted). But as this does not represent the pure fatty acid, but simply the hydrate of it (fatty acid + water), it is next necessary to subtract this amount of hydrated water from it, which is 3.25 per cent. for tallow, as well as for palm and cocoa butter.

The following process will indicate the amount of fat contained in a soap: if, for instance, 60 grains remain after the weight of wax has been deducted from the fatty cake, we have to bring those 3.25 per cent. in calculation. This will give us the number, 58.05. 80 grains of soap contain, therefore,

$$\frac{100 + 58.05}{80} = 72.8 \text{ per cent. fat.}$$

The existence of otherwise than saponified fat cannot be chemically ascertained with exactitude, but is easily to be detected by handling.

(c.) *Determination of the Amount of Rosin.*—If rosin be present it can be readily ascertained by a peculiar after-test. For the quantitative determination it has been proposed to dissolve, in cold alcohol, the fatty acids obtained by the decomposition of a solution of soap with diluted sulphuric acid; the alcohol dissolves chiefly the fat and leaves the rosin undissolved, which then should be dried and weighed. We only will remark that the fat obtained by decomposing the soap with the acid (no admixture of wax can be allowed in this case), should be carefully separated from the acid liquid, brought on a filter, and washed frequently with alcohol. The filter, with the rosin, should then be dried in a warm place. This method, however, does not give entire satisfaction with regard to exactitude, for it only approximatively shows the amount of rosin. Cailletet, apothecary, in Charleville, France, states that when a solution of rosin soap is shaken with dilute sulphuric acid and turpentine, a separation of the rosin takes place, which floats below the turpentine as a voluminous layer. Soap containing only 5 per cent. of rosin produces, by this treatment, a very distinct separation. Mr. Sutherland has lately, also, made known a new method for estimating resin in soaps, which is said to give most perfect results.

300 grains of soap, cut into small pieces, are placed into a capsule and covered with strong hydrochloric acid, the capsule being covered with a piece of glass and the contents kept gently boiling till the soap is dissolved and thoroughly decomposed; 3 or 4 ounces of hot water are then added, and the capsule is set aside to cool. When cold, the cake of fatty and resinous acids is carefully removed and remelted in pure water to remove any acid solution adhering. After cooling, it is dried on bibulous paper, and again very gently remelted and carefully brought to the boiling-point for a minute or two to expel the last traces of moisture.

This cake, containing the fatty and resinous acids, must now be weighed and the weight carefully noted.

100 grains of the mixed acids are placed in a 6 or 8 ounce capsule. It is covered with strong nitric acid, and the temperature gradually raised to the boiling-point, when a powerful action takes place with violent evolution of nitrous acid fumes. The heat is withdrawn till the violence of the action subsides, and is then again applied to maintain gentle ebullition for some minutes with frequent stirring. Small portions of nitric acid are successively added till no further distinctly appreciable quantity of nitrous acid is given off. The fatty acids are now allowed to cool, and are carefully removed from the strongly acid and richly colored solution of terebic acid. The cake is then washed by melting in a further quantity of nitric acid. When cold, it is dried and remelted at a gentle heat till acid fumes cease to be given off. The resulting cake is the

pure fatty acid freed from resin, the latter being, of course, indicated by the loss. It will be observed that a correction must be made to obtain the exact relative proportions of fat and resin originally put into the soap-pan, as fats, on being decomposed, lose about 4½ per cent. of their original weight—*i. e.*, 100 parts tallow—glycerine = 95½ parts fatty acid. Hence, in making our calculation, a proportionate addition must be made to the fatty acid before dividing its weight by that of the resin indicated. This process is also applicable to the estimation of resin as an adulteration of beeswax.

(*d.*) *Determination of the Amount of Alkali.*—A quantity of soap-scrapings, equal to that used in the former experiments, should be taken and put in a glass flask with a long neck and wide mouth; 3 ounces of absolute alcohol should then be added and the whole heated in the water-bath to the boiling-point. The true soap, as well as the free fat and free rosin, if any, are thereby solved, and the adulterative substances remain undissolved. The liquid should then be filtered hot, the residue on the filter washed with hot alcohol, and the filtered liquid evaporated in a porcelain capsule at a slow heat. Should there, however, be any carbonate of ammonia* in the soap, it will be recognized by the smell, being volatilized at a slow heat. After the vaporization of the alcohol, the remaining concentrated liquid should be diluted with water, so that any free fat or rosin may be brought to

---

* It is contained in the so-called tar soap of the Electric Soap Company, in New York, together with borax and acetate of lead.

the surface. The filtered liquid only contains the fat soap with the saponified rosin, if there be any. In order to estimate the quantity of the alkaline base, we refer the reader to our previous chapter, "Alkalimetry."

It yet remains to be determined whether the alkali be potash or soda. Soft soaps, and particularly semi-hard soaps, sometimes contain soda; and hard soaps, potassa. A quantitative determination of these substances, where a well-furnished chemical laboratory and skill in analysis are wanting, can only be obtained after many years' experience; hence we cannot give any detailed description here to find out the amount of these bases. We will only mention that bichloride of platinum produces in the neutral and acid solutions of the salts of potassa, a yellow crystalline, heavy precipitate, which in dilute solutions is only formed after some time. The best method of applying this reagent is consequently to evaporate the alcoholic solution of the potassa salt with the bichloride of platinum nearly to dryness on the water-bath, when if any potassa be present, it will surely show itself.

Soda is recognized, when after heating the aqueous or alcoholic solution of it in a porcelain capsule, and adding alcohol and igniting it, the flame appears strongly yellow.

A good soap, however, whatever may be the nature of the fat employed in its preparation, will not contain more than 10 per cent. of alkali; should there be more, *free* alkali is unquestionably present.

(*e.*) *Estimation of the Substances with which a Soap may be Adulterated to the Disadvantage of Consumers.*—For a more intelligible explanation of the substances with which a soap may be mixed, we will enumerate them in groups.

Group I.	Group II.		Group III.	
Water.	*Earthy Matters and Salts.*		*Organic Matters.*	
	Soluble and Insoluble in Water.		Soluble and Insoluble in Water.	
	Soluble.	Insoluble.	Soluble.	Insoluble.
	Chloride of Sodium. Soda. Glauber Salt. Borax. Soluble Glass.* Carbonate of Ammonia. Alum. Acetate of Lead.	*Soluble in Hydrochloric Acid.* MAGNESIA. LIME. CHALK. BONE ASHES. PIPE CLAY. *Not Soluble in Hydrochloric Acid.* SULPHATE OF BARYTES. SAND.†	Sugar. Starch.‡ Dextrin. Glue.	Free Resin. Free Fat.

With regard to the determination of the purposely increased amount of water, a description has been given. An admixture of carbonate of ammonia will be found at the determination of the amount of alkali, when the alcoholic soap solution is evaporated. Free fat and rosin are brought to the surface by concen-

* An admixture of soluble glass may be serviceable in some cases, provided a certain limit be not exceeded.

† An admixture of sand cannot be regarded as fraud if the soap is *sold* as *sand soap*.

‡ We do not know if starch has any cleansing qualities; it is so stated in a report on the different uses of the potato, published in 1827 by the two French chemists, Payen and Chevalier, but we doubt it.

trating this alcoholic liquid, and diluting it with water. With these exceptions, all the substances enumerated under Groups II and III, remain undissolved when the soap-scrapings are treated with absolute alcohol (for this process see (*d*)), and its amount may be ascertained by drying and weighing it.

If this residue is treated with boiling water, all the remaining organic and inorganic materials will be solved, except those in capitals. The solution obtained (designated C), is filtered. The remainder A is put aside. Chloride of sodium is found in the solution C, if nitrate of silver produces a white, curdy precipitate; lead is indicated, if sulphide of ammonium produces a black one; sugar will be recognized by its taste; starch and dextrin by the production of a blue color, and if tincture of iodine be added; glue by its peculiar odor, when a part of the solution is evaporated to dryness and burned.

In regard to the other substances which may be present in the filtered liquid C, and in the residue A, we cannot enter into any detailed description, upon the grounds already mentioned. Besides, to the practical savonnier it will not be of much consequence what foreign ingredients there are in soaps, if he only knows their quantity. We may, however, mention in conclusion, that if the remainder A be treated with muriatic acid, sand and sulphate of barytes will remain untouched, and if effervescence be produced, chalk is surely present.

PART III.

ON THE MANUFACTURE OF CANDLES.

THE MANUFACTURE OF CANDLES.

HISTORICAL.—FUNCTIONS OF THE CANDLE AS AN ILLUMINATOR.

From the works of Roman authors, as Pliny and Livius, the Romans were doubtless acquainted with illuminating materials, somewhat resembling our candles. We learn, in substance, from the above writers, that a kind of soaked wicks, similar to the torches frequently used at the present time for street illuminations, was known and employed in their day,—that the fat-dipped marc of rushes was used for placing at night near unburied dead bodies, and that the fibre of the flax served as a wick material. We cannot, however, discover from these authors what sort of lighting material was employed for soaking the stiff rush marc or the adhesive cord-wicks. Though Pliny furnishes us with a description of the beeswax and the method of bleaching it, as also of rendering tallow,—he does not state that these substances were used for illuminating purposes. Beckman in his "History of Inventions," tells us that by order of the Emperor Constantine, Byzanz, at the commencement of the fourth century, was illuminated on Christmas eve with lamps and wax candles; and Apuleius notices a distinction between wax and tallow candles (*cerei* and *sebacei*).

In the middle ages, wax candles and torches were employed for religious and private purposes. These seem to have been manufactured first in the houses of the wealthy, but subsequently became commodities of a regular trade. It seems, too, that previous to the invention of the clock, the burning-time of wax candles of a definite length and thickness, like the sand-glass, served for the approximate determination of time. The wax candle makers soon formed a very extensive class of operatives, and, from numerous documents, it is furthermore evident that they were in the habit of enveloping dead bodies in wax. Cierges and flambeaux were made in Venice during the seventeenth century, and the art of preparing them was thence introduced into Paris; but though in the latter period of the last century better products, similar to those of the present day, were manufactured, very imperfectly prepared illuminators, representing our candle, were yet in use. According to Gilbert White, rush-marc candles were made and used in 1775 in Hampshire, England; yet, as a reporter states, they emitted a light which was nothing but "visible darkness."

Mould candles, such as are now used, originated from Le Brez, of Paris, and were long ago in a more or less perfect state used as an illuminating material by the middle classes. The fact that rush-marc candles were also in use, is not more characteristic than that pine splinters are at this time employed in the spinning-rooms of the *Forest Noir*.

So long as candle-making had solely for its objects the formation of candles from certain crude materials, the products of nature, little, if any, improvement could be anticipated until energetic investigations were made with the laudable view of producing from the ordinary suet a harder and less fusible composition. These were partially pursued at the close of the last century, but restricted to the separation of the solid glycerides of the palmitine, and the stearine from the oils by pressing the melted and resolidifying fats.

Bolts first manufactured candles from pressed tallow in 1799. The art, however, of preparing by chemical means fatty bodies of excellent hardness from inferior materials (either by saponification or distillation), such as the palmitic and stearic acids, and the introduction of new substances, such as spermaceti and paraffine, belongs to the present progressive century.

THE FUNCTIONS OF THE CANDLE AS AN ILLUMINATOR.

These are not so simple as they appear. The candle, says F. Knapp in his "Chemical Technology," may be considered as a real microcosm of illumination, in which all the individual functions regulate each other. Whilst, for instance, the lamp is supplied already with a liquid lighting material, to be raised and regulated either by construction or mechanism, we see, in observing a burning candle, these operations performed by itself, and the melting of the lighting material as well as the absorption of the fused fat by the wick. We can furthermore discern its decomposition into gaseous products, and these are burning under circumstances most favorable for the evolution of light. If, for instance, the capacity of the wick is insufficient to absorb the melting of the candle stock, the excess will run over and form gutters, which interfere with the illumination; whilst, on the other hand, if the entire candle material, transformed into gas, cannot burn, a thick smoky flame will be the result. Again, should soot be collected in the interstices of the wick, its power of absorption will be impaired and the flame diminished in its clearness and brightness; in fact, there are many conditions to be fulfilled in order to produce a uniform, steady, and clear flame.

As the time necessary for liquefying wax, tallow, or stearic acid, depends chiefly on their respective melting-points, it is obvious that flames of equal magnitude and nearness will melt and consume more tallow than wax, the melting-point of the former being from 36° to 42° lower than that of the latter, or of stearic acid. In regard, however, to our ordinary candles, this is not the case, and the cause is obvious. If we look horizontally at the edge of a regularly burning stearine candle, the basis of the flame can be seen immediately above the edge. In the tallow candle, however, the basis of the flame is distinct from the edge, and a piece of uncharred wick, several lines in length intervenes. The wick of the tallow candle is also thicker and more saturated with liquid fat than that of the stearine candle, in which we can notice a well-formed reservoir filled with melted fat, but in the tallow candle this reservoir or hollow cup is not clearly marked. In the combustion, moreover, of a tallow candle, the liquid fat is obliged to rise higher by capillary attraction, so that the flame being more distant, the heat is necessarily lessened.

Were we to give to the tallow candle a wick of the same thickness as that used for a stearine or wax candle, the flame would burn nearer the fat,—the excessive heat causing it to melt more rapidly, would occasion an incessant guttering. Hence it is evidently requisite to supply tallow candles with proportionably thicker and more absorbing wicks than those used for candles made of a less fusible material. The capillary effects of the wicks, we may here remark, are considerably diminished, when a deposit of carbon is formed at the top, and it is well known that such a deposit is a very common occurrence in the tallow candle flame. Nor is this all, for in consequence of the oxygen of the air not coming sufficiently in contact with the thick and stiff wick of these candles, its combustion is not systematically effected, whilst its clearness is necessarily diminished from time to time. It is not so, however, with the twisted wicks of other candles, because as soon as the wick acquires a certain length, it bends downwards, and coming in contact with the air, is entirely consumed, thus obviating the frequent necessity of snuffing.

The wick of the candle, moreover, possesses an excellent, perhaps the only possible means for establishing an equilibrium between the amount of the generated inflammable gases, and that of the air necessary for combustion. Suppose we ignite a stick of candle without wick, the whole section of fat would be on fire at once, and a large portion of the burning material would thus be inaccessible to the oxygen of the atmosphere, but generating a large quantity of carbon, would emit a very dark smoky flame.

CHAPTER I.

ON THE RAW MATERIALS.

In its natural state, fat of animals is always associated with cellular tissue and other foreign matters, which must be separated before it can be used as candle stock. In all cases, this is done by heat, and the process is termed *rendering*. Partly by the melting of the fat globules, and partly by the transformation of moisture into steam, the tissues burst. By further heating the fibres of the cellular tissues contract, condensing the whole mass into a more compact form, and thereby facilitating the separation of the fat globules. There are different processes for the accomplishment of this rendering, which we proceed to describe for the benefit of those chandlers who prefer refining their own stock. By

THE OLD PROCESS,

called "*dry melting*" (much practised by small manufacturers), the rough suet is cut into coarse pieces and exposed to the action of a moderate heat. By the more recent processes, the fat is not exposed to heat till it has been subjected to certain mechanical and chemical appliances, for the purpose of destroying the tissues. The first-named method, we may observe, possesses this decided advantage, viz., that the residue or cracklings can be profitably used as food for hogs, fowls, &c. There is, moreover, an economy in fuel, while the simplicity of the process commends itself to the notice of inexperienced manufacturers. Disadvantages, on the other hand, arise and should be noted, viz., an obnoxious smell emanating from the heating of rough tallow, which has been collected and suffered to remain till it has become rancid, and the cellular tissues, blood, or other portions, advanced towards putrefaction. Fat from animals recently slaughtered does not, however, yield any very unpleasant effluvia. Another and more important disadvantage, in an economical point of view, is found in the smaller amount of fat obtained, as portions always remain with the cracklings when heated in this manner. The first care of the chandler should be to impress on the mind of his tallow merchant the importance of a more careful treatment of the rough suet than is generally observed by the butcher. The fat ought to be freed from the membranous and muscular parts as much as possible, then cut into thin slices and hung up in a cool place, *not heaped up while yet warm.* By operating thus, the disagreeable odor existing before melting, and increased during the process to an unbearable degree, can, at least, be delayed for several days.

First, the fat is chopped, for which purpose cutting machines are often used similar to the straw-cutting table; sometimes a thin, sharp-edged mince-hatchet is employed, about two and a half feet in length. This is held with both hands, and the fat, spread out on a beech block, is chopped into small pieces in all directions. A third instrument in vogue is a kind of stamp trough with muller, having a sharp blade in the form of an S, a contrivance frequently adopted for cutting beets. A more desirable and valuable instrument, however, is the ordinary rotary sausage-cutter, now in general use. The fat is then placed in melting caldrons (hemispherical in form, and, in this country, made of cast iron), which are heated by open fire. These caldrons are covered with movable tin plate hoods, so adjusted that, by means of pulleys, ropes, and counter-weights, they can be easily raised or lowered, whilst at the same time they serve to carry off the offensive vapors arising from the heated fat. Water is sometimes mixed with the fat in the caldrons, and this addition is specially beneficial when the fat has been long kept during the summer months, and thereby lost its natural moisture by evaporation. By gradually raising the temperature in the pan, the fat runs from the cells, and the whole is kept boiling from one to one and a half hours. The mixture of water with the fat-bubbles imparts to the liquid a milky appearance, but as soon as the water is volatilized, the fat becomes clear. During the whole operation of melting and boiling, the ingredients must be constantly and thoroughly stirred in order to keep the fat and cracklings in incessant agitation, otherwise pieces of unmelted suet, coming in contact with the sides or bottom, would become scorched and acquire a brownish tint, of which the whole melting would necessarily partake. Scorched tallow, it should be mentioned, is not very readily whitened. For separating the melted fat from the cracklings, it is ladled off from the caldron into a fine willow basket, or a copper box perforated at the bottom with innumerable small holes, set over large copper coolers, and allowed to remain undisturbed till all foreign matters (should it contain any), have settled down. Before it congeals, it should be transferred into small wooden pails.

This operation is continued so long as the cracklings yield any fat; and during the process, the heat must be maintained at a moderate temperature, to avoid scorching the materials. When the cracklings begin to harden, they acquire a darkish tint, and hence are said to be *browning*. They are then pressed, and the fat thus obtained possesses somewhat of the brown color of the cracklings, but not so much as to render it unfit for use as soap stock; it may, consequently, be mixed with that which has spontaneously separated while heating.

NEW METHODS OF RENDERING.

The complaints of parties residing in the neighborhood of candle and soap works, in consequence of the offensive effluvia disseminated by these establishments, have led to the invention of new apparatus, as well as to the introduction of new processes of rendering, until an entire reformation has resulted in the melting process, which we propose briefly to describe, long experience having demonstrated their utility.

No doubt the apparatus invented by d'Arcet, of Paris, in 1834, and introduced by the board of health of that city, has been tested in other places, where it did not interfere too much with the workmen's freedom of action, and the ready supervision of the melting process. As it is, moreover, applicable, and may prove serviceable in other branches of manufacture, we here venture to offer a few remarks relative to this invention.

PROCESS OF D'ARCET.

One essential and valuable feature in his invention is his suggestion for conducting the rising vapors, consisting chiefly of hydrogen and carbon, through channels under the grate of the rendering pan, and using them as fuel. The pan is also covered with a strong iron plate, the front third of which can be lifted by means of a knuckle whenever it is necessary for stirring, filling, or emptying the kettle. D'Arcet was, likewise, the first who employed certain chemicals for the purpose of neutralizing or destroying the noisome effluvia arising from the pans. His propositions are found to be, as yet, the most valuable in use. In the process recommended by him, 50 parts, by weight, of diluted acid (oil of vitriol), are first put into the kettle, then 1000 parts, in weight, of chopped fat are gradually added in four equal portions; and lastly, 150 parts of water, to which 5 parts in weight of sulphuric acid of 66° B., have been previously added. The whole is next heated. Under the influence of the acid, which partly destroys, partly solves the membranes, the rendering of even greater amounts of fat is effected in 1¼ to 2½ hours; two hours, however, are seldom required. The inventor's proposition of using acids was made when pans were heated by the direct action of the fire; but now, for various substantial reasons, steam is more generally employed. This, however, does not prevent the gases arising from the pans being thrown into the furnace and thereby aiding cumbustion. It is obvious, moreover, that in the boiler of d'Arcet, stirring, as well as filling or emptying the contents of the pan, cannot be accomplished so readily as in an open pan; nor can these processes be performed without opening the covers, when the noisome vapors escape into the room, to the annoyance of the operators. To obviate this, a contrivance similar to that used by distillers in the mashing process, could be introduced with decided advantage of comfort, as well as of certainty, for keeping up the necessary motion, to prevent adhesions to the sides or bottom of the vessel, and consequent incidental scorching.

The same may be said in regard to the pan for boiling fats lately patented in this country by W. H. Pinner, who yet claims the conducting of the noxious vapors into the fire as a *novelty.* With reference to the apparatus of d'Arcet, Mr. Morfit states that it is objectionable, inasmuch as there is danger of a conflagration from a too rapid flow of the vapors from the digester. Such an accident, however, has not yet occurred, and is probably more hypothetical than real. We may here further remark, that where steam is employed, the pans can be kept shut, and there will then be no danger of scorching.

Wilson's Process

has first been described by Prof. Campbell Morfit in his "Treatise on the Manufacture of Soap and Candles." The chief feature of this process is to steam the rough suet for ten or fifteen hours in a perfectly tight tank, under a pressure of fifty pounds to the square inch, or more when lard is being rendered. A higher pressure, according to Mr. Morfit, is not profitable, for, though expediting the process, it produces an inferior quality of fat. No chemicals are used. The apparatus, as patented by the inventor, consists of an upright cylindrical vessel, made of strong boiler plates, tightly riveted together. Its diameter is about two and a half times less than its height, and its capacity amounts to 1200 to 1500 gallons. It has a false bottom or diaphragm, below this a pipe enters, which is connected with an ordinary steam boiler. There is a man-hole at the top through which the vessel is filled with the rough suet or lard to within about two and a half feet of the top. By a safety-valve, the pressure can be regulated. There are, also, some try-cocks, by which the state of the contents can be examined; if the quantity of condensed steam in the tank be too great, it will be indicated by the ejection of the fatty contents at the top one. There is, moreover, a regulating cock at the bottom for drawing off the condensed steam as well as cocks in the side of the digester, by which the fatty materials can be drawn off. Through a hole made in the diaphragm, which can be shut and opened at will, the residual matters can be let out.

According to Morfit, the material obtained by this process (very much adopted in the Western States), is so far superior, that it always commands, if not the preference, at least a slight advance of price in the market. The difficulty, however, of separating all the water, slightly endangers the purity of the fat, as the former, in solution, introduces a portion of animal matter, which in time becoming putrescent, imparts an offensive odor to the latter. It is said, we may here observe, that repeated washing will materially remedy this defect.

FOUCHÉ'S PROCESS

is one of the most perfect. Fig. 9 represents a vertical, and Fig. 10 a horizontal section of the apparatus, as used by the inventor, after the line 1—2 in Fig. 9. Fig. 11 is a transverse section after the line

Fig. 9.

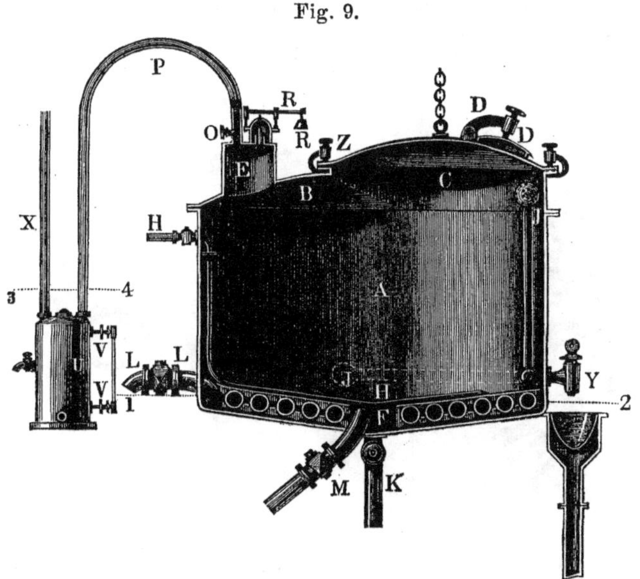

3—4 in the same figure. The vessel A has a copper dome B, fastened by rivets. In this dome is a hole C for introducing fat, having a cover, which may be lifted by a chain going over a pulley, and the margin of the cover may be fastened to the vessel by clamps. This cover has a hole for observing the inside, which can be shut by a valve fastened to the lever D. E is a cap on the dome with the eduction-pipe for vapors, and P P is a safety-valve, with a counter-weight R. There is, moreover, an outer valve for the passage of air, either when filling or emptying the vessel, as well as a box for a thermometer. The vapors escaping through P (which may be opened by the faucet O), pass into U for the purpose of being condensed there, or when not condensed, for escaping through X. F is a worm, which, fastened to the stays G (Fig. 10), lies

Fig. 10.

Fig. 11.

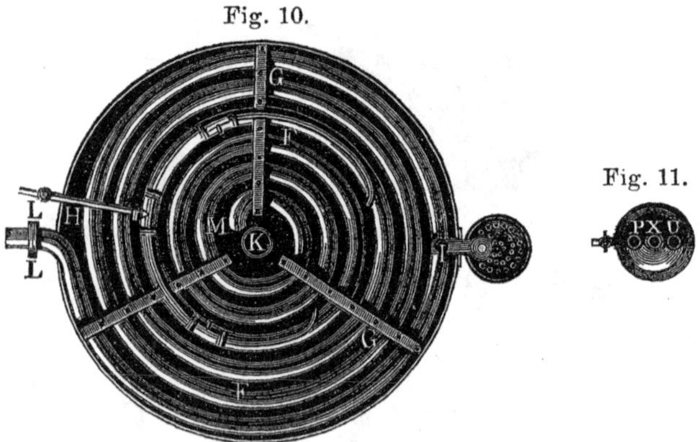

on the bottom of the vessel. Through L L steam is introduced from a boiler, and through M passes back into the same boiler. H H is a small pipe entering into the vessel A, through which steam also passes into the vessel, mainly for the purpose of keeping the melted fat in agitation. J is a tube, having a sieve at its upper end, and a movable crank below, by which it is fastened to the faucet Y. If the vessel is being emptied, the tube J is gradually let down until its upper part, with the sieve, reaches the bottom. The fat is then passed through J and Y, and through a fine sieve outside the vessel, which acts as a filter. In the above explained apparatus, 1000 lbs. are first introduced with 80 lbs. of water; $2\frac{4}{10}$ lbs. of sulphuric acid of 66 degrees, previously mixed with 16 lbs. of water, are then added. Steam is next turned on, which, as described, passes from the generator through the worm, and must have a tension of three atmospheres, *i. e.*, a temperature of 255° F. In the vessel, however, a tension of one and a half atmosphere is sufficient, and when this is reached, the safety-valve is no longer charged with weights. The vapors formed in the vessel are conducted through X into the hearth of the steam boiler furnace, so that all the noxious odors, which, however, by the action of the sulphuric acid, are diminished, but not destroyed, are thus conveyed from the working-rooms.

Evrard's Process.

In its features, the apparatus used by this inventor, very much resembles that of Wilson. The process, however, is based on the application of caustic lye, in the proportion of 25 gallons (each containing $\frac{1}{10}$ to $\frac{1}{7}$ lbs. of solid caustic soda) to every 250 to 350 lbs. of rough tallow. It is the object of the application of the lye, as in d'Arcet's process, to dissolve the membranous parts, so that no preliminary mincing be necessary. For boiling the fat, steam is employed. As the alkaline lye is heavier than water, it will also, after the boiling is completed, more easily subside. It is then drawn off, and the fat left in the tank is again boiled with successive portions of fresh water, for the better separation of which, this compound is left for twenty-four hours in a warm liquid state before being drawn off into the coolers.

It is stated by the most credited experimental reporters, that Evrard's process is better adapted for fresh fat of good quality, than for the medium and inferior kind. It is furthermore stated, that the former yields a very handsome and white product, with scarcely any noxious vapors observable, whilst the latter, when treated by this process, yields a dingy product, with the usual offensive odor. For this inferior kind, therefore, the treatment with sulphuric acid is preferable. Evrard's process, moreover, according to Stein, has these additional defects,—the boiling mass scums considerably, and certain fats, especially such as have already commenced to putrefy, are with difficulty separated from the lye.

Stein's Process.

This process has only recently been made public. If it accomplishes what the inventor claims, and being both simple and not costly, it will soon supersede all others, and, under any circumstances, will be a valuable supplementary. A mixture of slacked lime and small pieces of fresh-burnt charcoal is prepared, and spread upon a coarse cloth stretched over a hoop, of two inches in depth, and the circumference corresponding with the size of the pan. During the process of rendering, it is securely adjusted by suitable catches above the pan. The rising vapors from the latter, in necessarily passing this chemico-mechanical arrangement, are said to be entirely absorbed, so that thus all cause of complaint against tallow factories as health-destroying nuisances, would be effectually removed.

THE YIELD IN RENDERING.

According to Payen, the dry melting produces from 80 to 82 per cent. of clear fat, and the melting with steam from 83 to 85 per cent.

According to Gaultier de Glaubry, the dry melting furnishes 81.3 per cent., and the method of D'Arcet, with steam, 85 to 86 per cent., but only 81.2 to 84.2 if conducted on free fire.

Wilson's process of rendering, according to Morfit, yields 6 per cent. more than that obtained by an ordinary plan.

Faisst procured, by Evrard's process, 88 per cent. of white and inodorous fat, and subsequently an addition of 8 per cent. from the lye.

CLARIFYING TALLOW.

By mere melting and straining we do not obtain a fat entirely free from admixture of fine, undissolved substances. For separating these substances, therefore, it must be clarified. This is done by remelting it in water, either on free fire or by steam. Generally, no more water than 5 per cent. is taken, and stirred well with the fat till the mixture becomes emulsive. The whole is then allowed to rest, without further heating, till the water has separated, when the fat may be drawn off, or dipped off. Sometimes, in order to conceal the yellowish tint, a very little "blue color" is added to the clear fat, consisting of indigo rubbed finely with some oil, of which, a few drops are sufficient even for large quantities. The process of clarifying is occasionally repeated.

At the line of demarcation between the water and fat, a gray slimy substance is often perceptible, and the liquid itself is turbid. Instead of pure water, some tallow-melters take brine or solutions of alum, saltpetre, chloride of ammonium, or other salts. According to Dr. Orazio Lugo, these agents have no chemical action upon the fats, but simply induce a more rapid settling of the impurities and water, principally when strong agitation is used. Together with Dr. Lugo I have made experiments on several fatty oils, and we have obtained very satisfactory results by using substances with sharp angles in conjunction with strong agitation.

The yield, in melted tallow, necessarily depends upon the kind and quality of the rough suet. The fat enveloping the kidneys yields most, and fresh fat more than old. The quantity of cracklings by the dry process amounts to 4 per cent. when the process is well conducted and a good pressure afterward applied. These cracklings, when the fat is properly treated, are hard, nearly inodorous, and swell much in hot water. Besides animal fibre and blood, they always contain some fat, and splinters of wood from the cutting-blocks are also often found. Professor Bolley found that the cracklings produced by a very careful melting and pressing, contained 10 per cent. of fat.

Hardening of Tallow by Capaccionis' Process.

In 1000 parts of melted tallow, 7 parts of sugar of lead, previously dissolved in water, are stirred, during which process the mass must be constantly agitated. After a few minutes the heat is diminished, and 15 parts of powdered incense, with 1 part of turpentine added, under constant stirring of the mixture. It is then left warm for several hours, or until the insoluble substances of the incense settle to the bottom. The hardening is produced by the sugar of lead, yielding a material similar to the stearic acid, while the incense is improving its odor; it is also said that by this treatment the guttering or running of the candles is entirely prevented.

Cassgrand's Process for Bleaching Wax.

By this process, the bleaching of the wax by the sun and air is not prevented, but much time saved. The inventor first melts the wax with steam, which together pass through long pipes, so that a large surface becomes exposed to the steam. After traversing the pipes, it is received into a pan with a double bottom, heated by steam; it is therein treated by water, left quiet for some time until its impurities are settled. It is then forced anew through the pipe together with the steam, washed a second time, and, if necessary, this process is repeated a third time. Probably water is absorbed by the wax, thus rendering it more easily bleached.—The following is the arrangement of a bleachery:

Stakes or posts are driven into the ground, and two feet from the ground bag-clothes are stretched over them, or table-like frames are made from strips, and cloth stretched over the frames in the same manner as a sacking-bottom is stretched over a bedstead, care being taken to fasten the ends of the cords to the posts sufficiently firm as to prevent them loosening by the wind. This done, the wax ribbons are spread upon the cloth in a thin layer. It is important that the place selected for this arrangement be so that the sun's rays may have full play upon the exposed wax, but at the same time protected from the prevalent winds. The ribboned wax is daily turned over, in order that fresh portions of it may be affected by the sun, and should it not be sufficiently moistened by the dew or rain, soft water is poured over it. When it is not gradually becoming whiter, but still continues yellow upon the fracture, it is remelted, ribboned, and again bleached. The continuance of the bleaching process necessarily varies, depending, as it does, upon the weather; often one exposure to the sun and air suffices to bleach it, and no remelting is requisite. Four weeks are generally sufficient. The bleached wax is finally fused into cakes or square blocks, previously moistening the moulds. As fast as the wax congeals, the cakes are thrown into a tub of clean, cold water, and then taken out and spread upon a pack-thread sieve for draining. Eventually, they are dried and packed in boxes for the market, the loss being from 2 to 8 per cent.

CHAPTER II.

THE MANUFACTURE OF CANDLES.

Wicks.

As to what was used prior to the introduction of cotton for the manufacture of wicks, is merely a matter of curiosity. In the present day, we designate the wicks as twisted and plaited; the former, loosely twisted, and the fibre presents the appearance of a spiral similar to the separate strands of a rope; the latter, now generally adopted for most kinds of candles, is made by interlacing and crossing the strands of the wicks in the same manner as plaiting straw of bonnets. Common wicks are simply an aggregation of several loosely twisted threads forming one general cord of many fibres. This is effected by the ball winding machine, an apparatus of a very simple construction. More complicated machines, indeed, are used for the *plaiting* of wicks, but we do not deem it necessary to give any description of these in this work.

For *cutting* wicks, various machines are also applied. We proceed to describe Sykes's Apparatus, patented in England, and in very general use there, especially for tallow candle wicks, which must be soaked with tallow at one end.

Fig. 12 represents a vertical, and Fig. 13 a horizontal view of it. *c c* are spools on which the wicks are wound. *b* is a roller with grooves cut around it, by means of which the wicks are conveyed into the clamp *d* represented in Fig. 14 on a larger scale and as seen from the side. It consists of two wooden frames, which are made tapering from the middle towards the end. On each side there is a feather

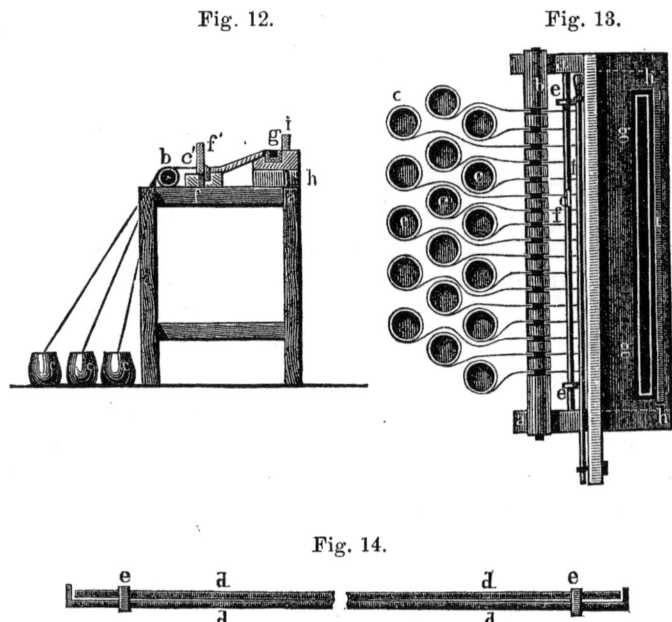

Fig. 12. Fig. 13.

Fig. 14.

of steel attached, for the purpose of holding the frames, with a space between them, which may be diminished by sliding the feathered clamps *e e* towards the middle, or increased by drawing them towards the end. Immediately behind the clamp there is a cutting apparatus, consisting of an immovable *f'*, and a movable blade *f*, with a handle. *g* is a small vessel filled with liquid fat (which may be kept from solidifying by steam), and a board *i* lying on the lathe *h*.

The use of the apparatus is as follows: the ends of the wicks, wound upon the spools *c c c*, are passed through the frame *d*, properly tightened by the clamps *e e*, so that all the wicks are kept firm. The knife *f* of the cutting apparatus is then lifted out of the way; the frame, with the wicks inclosed, is drawn backwards to the vessel *g*, and the ends of the wicks dipped in the melted fat; this done, the fat-soaked ends are drawn further back and placed under the weight I, which holds them firmly while the clamps are loosened on the frame, and this returned to its first described position and again tightened. The knife is next used, cutting all the wicks off at a stroke, then elevated, and the process repeated till a sufficient number of wicks are cut.

The thickness of the wicks, we may here remark, varies according to the diameter of the candles and the material of which they are made. The number of the cotton threads requisite to form a wick, also varies according to their firmness. Scarcely two chandlers, however, observe the same rules in these respects. The yarn is composed of a slack twisted cotton thread; No. 16 generally for plaited, and smaller, such as 8–12, for common wicks.

Bolley has published the appended index relative to the thickness of wicks. The yarn employed is No. 16.

For tallow candles,	per lb., the wick contains	threads.
For tallow candles,	8 per lb., the wick contains	42 threads.
"	7 "	45 "
"	6 "	50 "
"	5 "	55 "
"	4 "	60 "

These wicks, composed of 10, 12, or even 16 cords, are very loosely twisted, and form a kind of hollow tube.

For stearic candles, three-corded plaited wicks are generally used, smaller in size and of finer yarn. As, for instance—

Stearic candles,	per lb., the wicks consist of	threads.
Stearic candles,	4 per lb., the wicks consist of	108 threads.
"	5 "	96 "
"	6 "	87 "
"	8 "	63 "

In France, somewhat coarser kinds of yarn are employed for stearic candles, but wicks similar to the above are used for spermaceti and paraffine.

Preparing Wicks.

This is done by the so-called *wick-mordants*, by means of which they are less combustible, especially those for stearic acid, and composite candles prepared. For this purpose, compounds composed of solutions of ammoniac salts, of bismuth, of borates, or boracic acid, are used. Some of the receipts given in the journals and books devoted to technology are good as far as the *quality* of the substances is concerned, but not as regards the *quantity*. The recommended solutions are generally too strong. This may be said most assuredly of the following (Smitt's) preparations for wax candle wicks. He recommends 2 ounces of borax, 1 ounce of chloride of calcium, 1 ounce of nitrate of potash, 1 ounce of chloride of ammonium, to be dissolved in $\frac{3}{4}$ gallons of water, and afterwards dried.

A simple and cheap mordant for wicks, consists in a sal ammoniac solution of 2° to 3° B. This concentration is strong enough, and if a weaker one be used, a spark will remain on the wick after the candle has been blown out, and burning down to the fat, make relighting more difficult. Before moulding is performed, the wicks, having been saturated, are thoroughly dried in a tin box, surrounded by a jacket, in which steam is introduced. Instead of the sal ammoniac, phosphate of ammonia is used in some factories. A very good mordant is also a solution of $2\frac{4}{10}$ ounces boracic acid in 10 lbs. of water, with $\frac{1}{3}$ of an ounce of strong alcohol, and a few drops of sulphuric acid. Some mordants, we are aware, have become unpopular. The fault is in the nature of the crude cotton, which does not always readily become moistened; consequently, from not having completely imbibed the mordant, portions of the thread remain unsaturated, and are not equally combustible with the others. An admixture of alcohol will possibly remedy this defect, inasmuch as cotton is easier moistened in diluted spirit than in pure water.

Dips.

These candles are made by stringing a certain number of wicks upon a rod, and dipping them in melted tallow repeatedly. Though made in large quantities, they are only manufactured in comparatively small establishments. The process is very simple; it is as follows: The clarified and remelted tallow is poured into a tightly joined walnut or cherry trough, 3 feet long by 2 feet wide, and 10 to 12 inches wide at the top, gradually diminishing to 3 or 4 inches at the bottom. A handle is fixed on each end for its easy removal, and when not in use it is closed with a cover. The operator commences by stringing 16 to 18 wicks at equal intervals on a thin wooden rod, about 2½ feet long and sharpened at the ends. He then takes 10 or 12 such rods and dips the wicks rapidly into the fluid suet in a vertical direction. This suet should be very liquid, in order that the wicks be soaked as uniformly as possible, after which the several rods are rested on the ledges of the trough, when, if any of the wicks be matted together, they are separated, and the rods so placed on a frame, having several cross pieces, that the uncongealed tallow from the wicks may drop down, and while this is going on, which continues till the tallow is cooled and solidified, the operator is engaged in preparing another batch of rods. The fat in the trough, meanwhile, is so far cooled that in immersing the first dip again a thicker layer will adhere to the wicks. It is considered, we may observe, that when the suet solidifies at the sides of the vessel, the temperature is the most convenient for the object in view. It is, moreover, sometimes necessary to stir the ingredients to produce a uniform admixture, and in such cases much care should be taken so that no settlings be mingled with the mass, whilst by the addition of hot tallow any desired temperature may be obtained. The tallow on the wicks between each dipping becomes so gradually hardened, that at the third or fourth immersion new layers necessarily solidify; as a natural consequence of the method of dipping, the lower ends of the wicks become thicker than the upper, to remedy which the lower ends are again put into the melted fat for a few minutes, when the heat, as a matter of course, diminishes their dimensions. The process of dipping is continued until the candles acquire the requisite thickness. The conical spire at the upper end is formed by immersing *deeper* at the *last* dip, and if, eventually, the candles are too thick at the lower end, they are held over a slightly heated folded copper sheet, so that the fat may melt, but not be wasted.

"There are tricks," it is said, "in every trade," and many are practised in tallow candle making, but these we do not consider worth noticing in this book. For the purpose of saving time, many mechanical arrangements have been devised and completed, one of the most useful and used of which, involving the least outlay and requiring only one operator, is the EDINBURGH CANDLE-WHEEL, an apparatus already described by Ure and Morfit, and represented by Fig. 15.

The following is a description of it: A strong vertical post A is mounted on pivots, resting on a block T, and attached at the top in a beam P P, so that it can revolve freely on its centre. In the upright post A, six mortices are cut at short distances from each other, and crossing one another at an angle of 60 degrees. Each of these six mortises receives a bar D, which swings freely on a pin C, run through the centre of the bar E and post A. At the extremity of each bar is suspended a frame E (or port, as the workmen call it), containing six rods, on each of which are hung 18 wicks, making in all 1296 wicks on the wheel. As the bars B are all of the same length, and loaded with nearly the same weight, it is obvious that they will all naturally assume a hori-

Fig. 15.

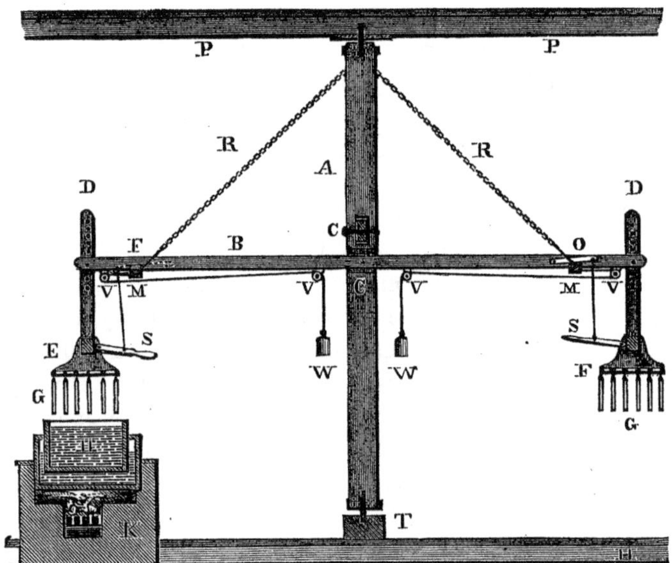

zontal position. In order, however, to prevent any oscillation of the machine when turning round, the levers are kept in a horizontal position by means of small chains R R, one end being fixed to the top of the upright shaft, and the other in a small block of wood M, which exactly fills the notch F. Notwithstanding its appearance, the machine is very easily turned round, and, when in motion, each port, as it successively passes over the tallow-kettle H, in its water-bath, mounted on a furnace K, is gently pressed downwards by the handle S. By these means, the wicks are regularly immersed in the tallow, and the square piece M (when the handle S is pressed down), is thrown out of the notch by the small lever O, inserted in the bar B. In order that, when the operator raises the port, the piece M may return to its proper position, a cord is attached to it, passing over the pulleys V V, and regulated by the weights W W. In the bars D several holes are bored, by means of which they may be heightened and lowered at will.

It may be readily perceived, therefore, with what regularity, ease, and expedition, the whole operation is performed (and that by one operator), the ports being not unnecessarily removed after each dip, and the process of congealing being much accelerated, as the candles are kept in constant motion through the air. Mr. Ure adds that, "in moderately cool weather not more than two hours are necessary for a single person to finish one wheel of candles of a common size," and that if "six wheels" (an assumed day's work), "are completed in one day, no less a number than 7776 candles will be manufactured in that space of time by one workman."

Moulds.

For moulding, besides the common metal moulds (a mixture of tin and lead), moulds of glass are sometimes used. The former are slightly tapering tubes, varying in length and dimensions according to the size of the candle to be manufactured, and, when required, are arranged in regularly perforated wooden frames or stands, with the smaller end downwards, forming the upper or pointed part of the candle. At this smaller end, the wick, previously saturated in melted fat, is inserted, filling the aperture and passing up the centre, is fastened perpendicularly at the opposite, *i. e.*, the upper end of the tube, to which is attached a movable cover. The melted fat is then poured in, generally with a small can, but a tinned iron syphon is far better. It is requisite that the tallow should *completely* fill the mould, that it should remain uncracked on cooling, and should be easily removable from the moulds. This can, however, only be obtained when the fat at the sides cools more quickly than that in the interior, and when the whole candle is rapidly cooled. A cool season is, for this reason, far better, but a certain condition of the tallow, namely, that which it possesses at a temperature very near its melting-point, is absolutely necessary. According to Knapp, candle-makers recognize the proper consistence of the tallow for moulding by the appearance of a scum upon the surface, which forms in hot weather between 111° and 119° F., in mild weather at 108°, and in cold about 104°. The tallow is usually melted by itself, sometimes, however, over a solution of alum. The candles are most easily removed from the mould the day after casting, to be cut and trimmed at the base.

Moulding.

Moulding by hand is a very tedious operation, and only practised in the smaller factories; in more extensive establishments, where economy of time and labor is a consideration, machinery is employed. We here transcribe a recent American invention for the above purpose, viz.,

Kendall's Moulding Apparatus.

Fig. 16 represents a vertical transverse section through one of the mould frames, exhibiting the candles drawn from the moulds. Fig. 17 represents a top view of a row of moulds, showing the clamp in place ready to centre the wicks. The moulds are mounted upon cars, for being carried from place to place as required; each capable of conveying several dozens, which are heated to about the temperature of the melted fat by running the car into an oven. The moulds thus heated are carried by cars to a caldron containing the melted fat, with which they are filled. The car is then attached to one of the empty tracks and allowed to remain till the candles are cooled, when it is moved to an apparatus, by means of which the candles are drawn and the moulds rewicked, and again ready to be heated and filled.

To facilitate the transference of the moulds to different parts of the room, the cars on which they are mounted are carried about on trucks fitted with rails at right angles to the track on which they run, so that the car with the moulds can be carried forward or back by the truck, and run to the right or left on its own wheels upon lateral tracks at will.

In Fig. 16, *m m* represent moulds mounted on two horizontal boards *a* and *b* (in which round holes are cut) and tightly screwed at the upper end, around which a thin wooden frame is attached, three-fourths of which is firmly fastened, whilst the other one-fourth forms a slide. The lower end of the moulds rests on pieces of vulcanized India-rubber *o*, let into the cross-bar *e*; each piece of India-rubber being pierced with a hole somewhat smaller than the wick,

Fig. 16.

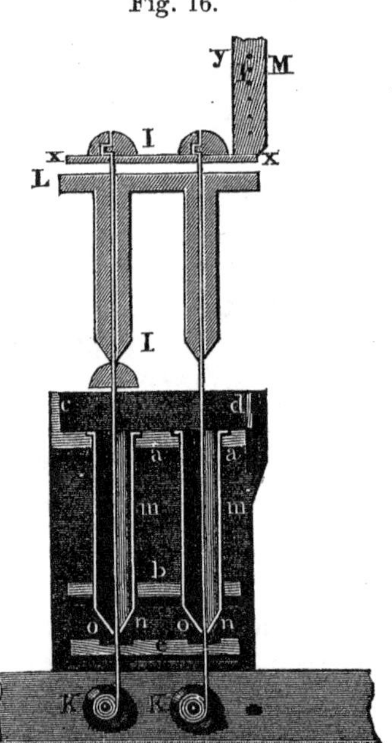

and as the wick is passed through this hole, the latter compresses it so tightly as to prevent the fat from leaking out. In like manner, the leakage is prevented between the bottom or tip *n* by the pressure of the mould upon the India-rubber. The spools K hold the wicks firmly and centrically secured by clamps, as seen in Fig. 17. On the ledge *c*, moreover, of the bottom *a* there are four pins *i*, which tighten the clamps *j* (Fig. 17) by means of small holes *g h*. On one side F of the clamp there are also toothed jaws, in which the wicks fit exactly, *i. e.*, they are thus kept vertical and in the *centre* of the moulds.

The construction of the clamp, Fig. 17, is such that the arm working upon a joint at *g* and being brought against the arm F, falls into a groove made in its length, so as to press and kink the wicks in said groove, and fasten them firmly there by means of the spring-catch K. The object of this is, that in raising the candles from the moulds by this clamp they shall not slip nor move. As the candles are

Fig. 17.

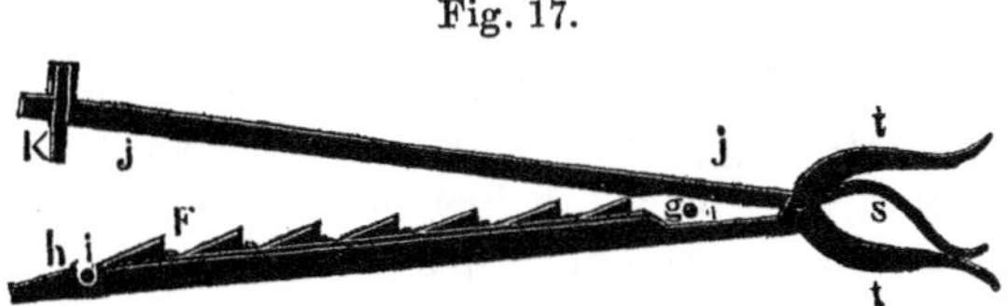

lifted out of the moulds (as in Fig. 16), the wicks are drawn after them from the spools K, and are then clamped in position in the manner described. The wicks are next cut off above the lower clamp, the candles with the clamps removed, when, by sliding off the spring-catch K, the spring S, between the jaws *t t*, causes the arms *j* F to separate and release the wicks.

Composite Candles.

Cérophane.—The mode for manufacturing this block is the following. Melt together, over a water-bath, 100 parts of stearic acid, and 10 to 11 parts of bleached beeswax; but to insure success, the mixture must remain over the bath for 20 to 30 minutes, and without being stirred or agitated. At the end of that time, the fire is to be extinguished, and the fluid allowed to cool until a slight pellicle is formed on the surface, when it is cast direct into the moulds, previously heated to the same temperature, but with the precaution of avoiding stirring the mixture, as a disregard of it would cause opaqueness of the mixture, instead of transparency.

Transparent Bastard Bougie, by Debitte, of Paris.—For 100 pounds of stock take 90 pounds of spermaceti, 5 lbs. purified suet of mutton, and 5 lbs. wax; melt each separately over a water-bath, and to the whole, when mixed together, add 2 ounces of alum, and 2 ounces of bitartrate of potassa in fine powder, and, while stirring constantly, raise the heat to 176° F., then withdraw the fire and allow the mixture to cool to the temperature of 140° F. When the impurities subside, the clear liquid must be drawn off into clean pans. For quality and good appearance, candles made of this cooled block are more than proportional to its cost. Prof. C. Morfit recommends to substitute plaited wicks for the foregoing mixture to the wicks generally used for composite candles, and to prepare them by previously soaking in a solution of 4 ounces borax, 1 ounce chlorate of potassa, 1 ounce nitrate of potassa, and 1 ounce sal ammoniac, in 3 quarts of water. After being thoroughly dried, they are ready for moulding.

Diaphane.—It is, like the block for cérophane, an invention of Boilot, and made by melting together, in a steam jacket, from 2½ to 17½ lbs. of vegetable wax, $1\frac{1}{2}$ to $10\frac{1}{2}$ of pressed mutton tallow, and 22 to 46 lbs. of stearic acid. Both the latter and the vegetable wax are the hardening ingredients. By changing the proportions between the above limits, a more or less consistent mixture may be formed. As concerns the moulding, it is performed in the same manner as for stearic acid candles.

Parlor Bougies, similar to Judd's "Patent Candles."—Although not bougies, a name which, properly speaking, is only applicable to candles of wax alone, the similarity of these candles to those of wax has induced the aforenamed title for them. According to Prof. Morfit, their mode of manufacture is as follows: Melt slowly, over a moderate fire, in a well-tinned copper kettle, 70 lbs. of pure spermaceti, and to it add piecemeal, and during constant stirring, 30 lbs. of best white wax. By increasing the proportion of wax to 50 lbs., the resulting product is much more diaphanous; however, the bougies moulded of this mixture are not as durable as candles made exclusively of wax. They are tinted in different colors. For red, carmine or Brazil-wood, together with alum, are used. Yellow is given with gamboge, blue with indigo, and green with a mixture of yellow and blue. Sometimes the bougies are perfumed with essences, so that in burning they may diffuse an agreeable aroma.

A still more transparent and elegant bougie is made by adding only $6\frac{1}{2}$ lbs. of wax to 100 lbs. of pure, dry sperm, and the candles made of the block formed in these proportions resemble very much the "patent candles" of Judd.

"*Composite Candles.*"—The block for these candles is made by adding a portion of hot-pressed cocoa-stearine to stearic acid of tallow. It is an excellent and economical mixture, in which the red, carbonaceous flame of the latter ingredient is improved in illuminating power by the white and more hydrogenated flame of the stearine.

"*Belmont Sperm.*"—It consists merely of a mixed stock of hot-pressed stearic acid, from palm and cocoa-butters. Palmitic acid colored by gamboge is called *Belmont wax.*

APPENDIX.

I.

AREOMETERS AND THERMOMETERS.

Areometers,

CALLED also hydrometers, are instruments for measuring the density or specific gravity of liquids, and constructed upon the theory that a floating body displaces a bulk of fluid equal to its own weight. When made for specific use, they have corresponding names, as the alcoholometer for spirits, the saccharometer for solutions of sugar, the lactometer for milk, the potassimeter for potassa, &c. The most common form of such instruments consists of a hollow cylindrical glass body terminating at its lower extremity in a bulb with mercury or shot, so as to maintain it in a vertical position, and a graduated elongation at its upper part, so as to enable one to note accurately the depth of its immersion.

The first requirement for such an instrument is, that it neither sinks entirely, nor rises with its whole tube above the surface of the fluid. Water is taken as the standard for comparison, and we express its specific weight with 1.000. If an areometer be constructed, adapted for either liquid denser or liquid lighter than water, it should float in the water at about the middle of the tube; less deep in denser, and more deep in lighter liquids, whilst in both cases only a part of the tube ought to rise above the surface.

An instrument fulfilling those requirements would obviously require a very long tube, rendering it not only extremely inconvenient, but also liable to be easily broken; hence, distinct areometers have been made, as for liquids denser, and for liquids lighter than water.

As the specific gravity of a liquid is determined for ascertaining its "strength" or the amount of valuable matter therein contained, it follows, that, fluids varying, we must have tables indicating the quantity *per cent.* corresponding with the specific gravity. If, for instance, by immersion of an hydrometer, we find the specific gravity of a lye of caustic potassa to be 1.047, *i. e.*, if the instrument sinks to that number, we require a table, founded on direct experiments, to show us how many per cent. of anhydrous potassa corresponds with it. Table III, on page 174, indicates that there are 5.002 per cent. of potassa in such lye. If, again, the same instrument notes in a solution of carbonate of soda 1.0708, Table VI teaches us that it contains 18 per cent. of crystallized, or 6.670 of anhydrous soda.

The theory, however, having been satisfactorily established, that a liquid of a specific strength has always a corresponding specific gravity, thus rendering tables, as above described, superfluous, instruments are now generally used, known as areometers *with a rational graduation.* For instance, it has been ascertained that an areometer in a solution of carbonate of soda of 18 per cent. will invariably sink to the number 1.0708; hence the percentage of the liquid is sufficiently expressed by the simple figure 18.

Hydrometers with *an empiric graduation*, contain a scale, divided into degrees of equal length. Of this kind is that of Baumé, and there are generally two of them in use, one for liquids denser, and another for liquids lighter than water. The former is constructed on the basis, that when, in distilled water, it shall sink to nearly the upper portion of the stem, this point being expressed with 0, and the point to which it sinks, when immersed in a solution of 15 parts of chloride of sodium, and 85 parts of water, being marked with 15, and the intervening space divided into 15 equal parts. Of these, about 50 are continued the length of the stem. The latter instrument, on the other hand, is constructed on the following basis: that when in a solution of 1 part of chloride of sodium and 9 parts water, it shall float to nearly the lower extremity of the stem, this point being marked with 0, and the point to which it sinks in distilled water expressed by the figure 10, and the intervening space divided into 10 equal parts, the tube being divided into as many of these as its length will admit. It is obvious, however, that in using an hydrometer, with an empiric graduation, we only obtain the relative densities of liquids of different strengths. A further calculation is required to ascertain what per cent. of material is necessary to produce with water a liquid of a given specific gravity. To avoid, however, the constant necessity of these calculations, tables have been prepared for various bases, showing the percentage of solid matter in an aqueous fluid for every degree marked by the instrument. Table I, for instance, is constructed for converting the areometric degrees of Baumé into the specific weights of liquids lighter, and Table II of liquids heavier than water.

These tables, are, indeed, invaluable, saving much time and calculation; for, suppose in a solution of carbonate of soda, the instrument indicates 31, it will at once be seen by Table II that this number corresponds with the specific weight of 1.256; and by Table IV that soda lye of this density contains 26 per cent. of carbonate of soda in solution.

Hydrometers made with a rational graduation, such as the alcoholometers and the saccharimeters, indicate the percentage of the pure material in solution at once by the scale. Solutions of different substances, however, may have, and do have, different amounts of pure material, and yet an entirely different density; consequently an hydrometer of this kind, prepared for one liquid, is not a measure of percentage for another. Hence, a different instrument is required for each kind of liquid to be tested.

Hydrometers, with a scale on which the specific weights are noted, may, however, be employed in every case, but then for every liquid, a table is required indicating the corresponding percentage. If areometers, with empiric scales, be used, we then need also tables, as those communicated for the areometer of Baumé, which for each degree of the scale indicate the specific gravity of the fluid tested.

As the density of all liquids is changed by heat, so the hydrometer must be constructed to be used at a certain defined temperature, and all liquids tested by it should be brought to that temperature, otherwise the result will be inaccurate. It is perhaps scarcely necessary to add that when testing the strength of a liquid, all foreign matters affect its density.

I. *Table for converting the Areometric Degrees of Baumé into the specific weights of Liquids lighter than Water.*

Temperature of liquid, 54° Fahr.

10	1.0000	23	0.9183	36	0.8488	49	0.7892
11	0.9932	24	0.9125	37	0.8439	50	0.7849
12	0.9865	25	0.9068	38	0.8391	51	0.7807
13	0.9799	26	0.9012	39	0.8343	52	0.7766
14	0.9733	27	0.8957	40	0.8295	53	0.7725
15	0.9669	28	0.8902	41	0.8249	54	0.7684
16	0.9605	29	0.8848	42	0.8202	55	0.7643
17	0.9502	30	0.8795	43	0.8156	56	0.7604
18	0.9480	31	0.8742	44	0.8111	57	0.7565
19	0.9420	32	0.8690	45	0.8066	58	0.7526
20	0.9359	33	0.8639	46	0.8022	59	0.7487
21	0.9300	34	0.8588	47	0.7978	60	0.7449
22	0.9241	35	0.8538	48	0.7935		

II. *Table for converting the Areometric Degrees of Baumé into the specific weights of Liquids heavier than Water.*

Temperature of liquid, 54° Fahr.

0	1.0000	18	1.1343	36	1.3003	54	1.5510
1	1.0066	19	1.1408	37	1.3217	55	1.6471
2	1.0133	20	1.1585	38	1.3333	56	1.6667
3	1.0201	21	1.1603	39	1.3451	57	1 6868
4	1.0270	22	1.1692	40	1.3571	58	1.7074
5	1.0340	23	1.1783	41	1.3694	59	1.7285
6	1.0401	24	1.1875	42	1.3818	60	1.7501
7	1.0483	25	1.1908	43	1.3845	61	1.7722
8	1.0556	26	1.2063	44	1.4094	62	1.7950
9	1.0630	27	1.2160	45	1.4206	63	1.8184
10	1.0704	28	1.2258	46	1 4339	64	1.8423
11	1.0780	29	1.2358	47	1.4476	65	1.8669
12	1.0857	30	1.2459	48	1 4615	66	1.8922
13	1.0935	31	1.2562	49	1.4758	67	1.9180
14	1.0994	32	1.2667	50	1.4902	68	1.9447
15	1.1095	33	1.2773	51	1.4951	69	1.9721
16	1.1176	34	1.2881	52	1.5200	70	2.0003
17	1.1259	35	1.2992	53	1.5353		

The following tables exhibit the percentage of various substances contained in solutions of different specific gravities.

III. *Table showing the Quantity of Anhydrous Potassa in Caustic Potassa Lye.*

Specific Gravity.	Potassa in 100.	Specific Gravity.	Potassa in 100.	Specific Gravity.	Potassa in 100.	Specific Gravity.	Potassa in 100.
1.3300	28.290	1.2268	20.935	1.1308	13.013	1.0478	5.002
1.3131	27.158	1.2122	19.803	1.1182	11.882	1.0369	3.961
1.2966	26.027	1.1979	18.671	1.1059	10.750	1.0260	2.829
1.2805	24.895	1.1838	17.540	1.0938	9.619	1.0153	1.697
1.2648	23.764	1.1702	16.408	1.0819	8.487	1.0050	0.5658
1.2493	22.632	1.1568	15.277	1.0703	7.355		
1.2342	21.500	1.1437	14.145	1.0589	6.224		

IV. *Gerlach's Table for the Quantity of Carbonate of Soda in its Solutions.*

Per cent.	Specific Weight.	Per cent.	Specific Weight.	Per cent.	Specific Weight.	Per cent.	Specific Weight.
1	1.00914	14	1.13199	27	1.26787	40	1.41870
2	1.01829	15	1.14179	28	1.27893	41	1.43104
3	1.02743	16	1.15200	29	1.28999	42	1.44338
4	1.03658	17	1.16222	30	1.30105	43	1.45573
5	1.04572	18	1.17243	31	1.31261	44	1.46807
6	1.05513	19	1.18265	32	1.32417	45	1.48041
7	1.06454	20	1.19286	33	1.33573	46	1.49314
8	1.07396	21	1.20344	34	1.34729	47	1.50588
9	1.08337	22	1.21402	35	1.35885	48	1.51861
10	1.09278	23	1.22459	36	1.37082	49	1.53135
11	1.10258	24	1.23517	37	1.38279	50	1.54408
12	1.11238	25	1.24575	38	1.39476	51	1.55728
13	1.12219	26	1.25681	39	1.40673	52	1.57048

V. *Table for the Quantity of Caustic Soda in Soda Lye.*

Specific Gravity.	Per cent.	Specific Gravity.	Per cent.	Specific Gravity.	Per cent.	Specific Gravity.	Per cent
1.4285	30.220	1.3198	22.363	1.2392	15.110	1.1042	7.253
1.4193	29.616	1.3143	21.884	1.2280	14.506	1.0948	6.648
1.4101	29.011	1.3125	21.894	1.2178	13.901	1.0855	6.944
1.4011	28.407	1.3053	21.154	1.2058	13.297	1.0764	5.540
1.3923	27.802	1.2982	20.550	1.1948	12.692	1.0675	4.835
1.3836	27.200	1.2912	19.945	1.1841	12.088	1.0587	4.231
1.3751	26.594	1.2843	19.341	1.1734	11.484	1.0500	3.626
1.3668	25.989	1.2775	18.730	1.1630	10.879	1.0414	3.022
1.3586	25.385	1.2708	18.132	1.1528	10.275	1.0330	2.418
1.3505	24.780	1.2642	17.528	1.1428	9.670	1.0246	1.813
1.3426	24.176	1.2578	16.923	1.1330	9.066	1.0163	1.209
1.3349	23.572	1.2515	16.319	1.1233	8.462	1.0081	0.604
1.3273	22.967	1.2453	15.814	1.1137	7.857	1.0040	0.302

VI. *H. Schiff's Table for the Quantity of Crystallized and Anhydrous Soda in Solutions of Carbonate of Soda.*

Specific Weight.	Per cent. of Crystallized Soda.	Per cent. of Anhydrous Soda.	Specific Weight.	Per cent. of Crystallized Soda.	Per cent. of Anhydrous Soda.
1.0038	1	0.370	1.1035	26	9.635
1.0076	2	0.741	1.1076	27	10.005
1.0114	3	1.112	1.1117	28	10.376
1.0153	4	1.482	1.1158	29	10.746
1.0192	5	1.853	1.1200	30	11.118
1.0231	6	2.223	1.1242	31	11.488
1.0270	7	2.594	1.1284	32	11.859
1.0309	8	2.965	1.1326	33	12.230
1.0348	9	3.335	1.1368	34	12.600
1.0388	10	3.706	1.1410	35	12.971
1.0428	11	4.076	1.1452	36	13.341
1.0468	12	4.447	1.1494	37	13.712
1.0508	13	4.817	1.1536	38	14.082
1.0548	14	5.188	1.1578	39	14.453
1.0588	15	5.558	1.1620	40	14.824
1.0628	16	5.929	1.1662	41	15.195
1.0668	17	6.299	1.1704	42	15.566
1.0708	18	6.670	1.1746	43	15.936
1.0748	19	7.041	1.1788	44	16.307
1.0789	20	7.412	1.1830	45	16.677
1·0830	21	7.782	1.1873	46	17.048
1.0871	22	8.153	1.1916	47	17.418
1.0912	23	8.523	1.1959	48	17.789
1.0953	24	8.894	1.2002	49	18.159
1.0994	25	9.264	1.2045	50	18.530

Thermometers

are instruments for the measurement of temperatures. As the imperfection of our senses does not enable us to determine the temperature of bodies, except so far as the impression of higher or lower temperature excites these sensations in us, it became necessary to have recourse to the physical effects of heat on certain bodies. Such effects are various, but being most easily observed, dilatations and contractions are generally adopted. Of all bodies, liquids are preferable for the construction of thermometers, as the solids are not sufficiently dilatable, and the gases too much so. Mercury and alcohol are exclusively employed; the first, because it does not boil but at a very high temperature, and the second because it does not solidify at the coldest point known. Mercury is generally used. The instrument is composed of a capillary glass tube, terminating in a cylindrical or spherical bulb of the same material. The reservoir and a part of the stem are filled with mercury, and by a scale, graduated on the tube itself, or on a board parallel to it, we ascertain the expansion of the liquid. On the stem, moreover, two fixed points are marked, representing always identical and easily reproducible temperatures. Now, experience has shown that the temperature of melting ice is invariably the same, whatever may be the source of heat, and that distilled water enters constantly in ebullition at a particular temperature, provided there be the same pressure, and in a vessel of the same material. Consequently, for the first point, *i. e.*, for the zero of the scale, the temperature of melting ice has been taken, and for the second the temperature of boiling distilled water. These two having been defined, the intervening space is divided into equal parts or degrees, and these divisions are continued the length of the scale.

We distinguish in the graduation of thermometers *three scales*, the Centigrade, Réaumur's, and Fahrenheit's; the first is much used in France, and by authors of scientific works in Europe, England excepted. It was invented by Celsius, a Swedish physician, who died in 1744. Réaumur, a French physician, constructed his in 1731, both adopting the same freezing and boiling points; whilst in the latter, the intervening space is divided into 80 degrees, so that 80 degrees Réaumur are equivalent to 100 degrees Centigrade. One degree R. is therefore equal to $\frac{100}{80}$ or $\frac{5}{4}$ degrees of Celsius, and, reciprocally, one degree C. is equal to $\frac{80}{100}$, or $\frac{4}{5}$ degrees R. Consequently, for converting a number of degrees R. into degrees C.—20 for instance—this number must be multiplied by $\frac{5}{4}$, because 1 degree R. is equal to $\frac{5}{4}$ degrees C. 20 degrees R. converted into C. are 20 times $\frac{5}{4}$, or 25. It is obvious, also, that for converting the degrees of C. into those of R. they must be multiplied by $\frac{4}{5}$.

Fahrenheit, in Danzik, Prussia, contrived, in 1714, a thermometrical scale, which is popular in Holland, England, and the United States, which, we may add, has been our guide in the present undertaking. The upper fixed point of this instrument corresponds with the boiling-point of water; but the *zero* corresponds to a temperature obtained by mixing equal parts of pulverized sal ammoniac and snow together, the intervening space being divided into 180 degrees.

The thermometer of Fahrenheit when placed in melting ice, marks 32°; consequently 100° Centigrade are equivalent to 212 minus 32 or 180; 1° C. is therefore equal to $\frac{180}{100}$, or $\frac{9}{5}$° F.; and, reciprocally, 1° F. is equal to $\frac{100}{180}$ or $\frac{5}{9}$° C.

Suppose a certain number of degrees Fahrenheit (say 85) have to be converted into degrees C. For this purpose, first, 32 must be subtracted from the given number, so as to count the two kinds of degrees from the same point of the stem. The remainder is 53. And, as 1° F. is equal to $\frac{5}{9}$° C., 53° are equal to $\frac{5}{9} \times 53 = 29\frac{4}{9}$ C. Reciprocally, for converting degrees of C. into degrees of F., the given number must be multiplied by $\frac{9}{5}$, and 32 added to the product.

We here affix tables showing the corresponding value of each scale:

VII. *Comparison between the Scale of Fahrenheit and those of Celsius and Réaumur.*

Fahrenheit.	Celsius.	Réaumur.	Fahrenheit	Celsius.	Réaumur.
+212	+100	+80	+171	+77.22	+61.78
211	99.44	79.56	170	76.67	61.33
210	98.89	79.11	169	76.11	60.89
209	98.33	78.67	168	75.55	60.44
208	97.78	78.22	167	75	60
207	97.22	77.78	166	74.44	59.56
206	96.67	77.33	165	73.89	59.11
205	96.11	76.89	164	73.33	58.67
204	95.55	76.44	163	72 78	58.22
203	95	76	162	72.22	57.78
202	94.44	75.56	161	71.67	57.33
201	93.89	75.11	160	71.11	56.89
200	93.33	74.67	159	70.55	56.44
199	92.78	74.22	158	70	56
198	92.22	73.78	157	69.44	55.56
197	91.67	73.33	156	68 89	55.11
196	91.11	72.89	155	68.33	54.67
195	90.55	72.44	154	67.78	54.22
194	90	72	153	67.22	53.78
193	89.44	71.56	152	66.67	53.33
192	88.89	71.11	151	66.11	52.89
191	88.33	70.67	150	65.55	52.44
190	87.78	70.22	149	65	52
189	87.22	69.78	148	64.44	51.56
188	86.67	69.33	147	63.89	51.11
187	86.11	68.89	146	63.33	50.67
186	85.55	68.44	145	62.78	50.22
185	85	68	144	62.22	49.78
184	84.44	67.56	143	61.67	49.33
183	83.89	67.11	142	61.11	48.89
182	83.33	66.67	141	60.55	48.44
181	82.78	66.22	140	60	48
180	82.22	65.78	139	59.44	47.56
179	81.67	65.33	138	58.89	47.11
178	81.11	64.89	137	58.33	46.67
177	80.55	64.44	136	57.78	46.22
176	80	64	135	57.22	45.78
175	79.44	63.56	134	56.67	45.33
174	78.89	63.11	133	56.11	44.89
173	78.33	62.67	132	55.55	44.44
172	77.78	62.22	131	55	44

TABLE VII.—*Continued.*

Fahrenheit.	Celsius.	Réaumur.	Fahrenheit	Celsius.	Réaumur.
+130	+54.44	+43.56	+85	+29.44	+23.56
129	53.89	43.11	84	28.89	23.11
128	53.33	42.67	83	28.33	22.67
127	52.78	42.22	82	27.78	22.22
126	52.22	41.78	81	27.22	21.78
125	51.67	41.33	80	26.67	21.33
124	51.11	40.89	79	26.11	20.89
123	50.55	40.44	78	25.55	20.44
122	50	40	77	25	20
121	49.44	39.56	76	24.44	19.56
120	48.89	39.11	75	23.89	19.11
119	48.33	38.67	74	23.33	18.67
118	47.78	38.22	73	22.78	18.22
117	47.22	37.78	72	22.22	17.78
116	46.67	37.33	71	21.67	17.33
115	46.11	36.89	70	21.11	16.89
114	45.55	36.44	69	20.55	16.44
113	45	36	68	20	16
112	44.44	35.56	67	19.44	15.56
111	43.89	35.11	66	18.89	15.11
110	43.33	34 67	65	18.33	14.67
109	42.78	34.22	64	17.78	14.22
108	42.22	33.78	63	17.22	13.78
107	41.67	33.33	62	16.67	13.33
106	41.11	32.89	61	16.11	12.89
105	40.55	32.44	60	15.55	12.44
104	40	32	59	15	12
103	39.44	31.56	58	14.44	11.56
102	38.89	31.11	57	13.89	11.11
101	38.33	30.67	56	13.33	10.67
100	37.78	30.22	55	12.78	10.22
99	37.22	29.78	54	12.22	9.78
98	36.67	29.33	53	11.67	9.33
97	36.11	28.89	52	11.11	8.89
96	35.55	28.44	51	10.55	8.44
95	35	28	50	10	8
94	34.44	27.56	49	9.44	7.56
93	33.89	27.11	48	8.89	7.11
92	33.33	26.67	47	8.33	6.67
91	32.78	26.22	46	7.78	6.22
90	32.22	25.78	45	7.22	5.78
89	31.67	25.33	44	6.67	5.33
88	31.11	24.89	43	6.11	4.89
87	30.55	24.44	42	5.55	4.44
86	30	24	41	5	4

TABLE VII.—*Continued.*

Fahrenheit.	Celsius.	Réaumur.	Fahrenheit	Celsius.	Réaumur.
+40	+4.44	+3.56	—1	—18.33	+14.67
39	3.89	3.11	2	18.89	15.11
38	3.33	2.67	3	19.44	15.56
37	2.78	2.22	4	20	16
36	2.22	1.78	5	20.55	16.44
35	1.67	1.33	6	21.11	16.89
34	1.11	0.89	7	21.67	17.33
33	0.55	0.44	8	22.22	17.78
32	0	0	9	22.78	18.22
31	0.55	0.44	10	23.33	18.67
30	—1.11	0.89	11	23.89	19.11
29	1.67	1.33	12	24.44	19.56
28	2 22	1.78	13	25	20
27	2.78	2.22	14	25.55	20.44
26	3.33	2.67	15	26.11	20.89
25	3.89	3.11	16	26.67	21.33
24	4.44	3.56	17	27.22	21.78
23	5	4	18	27.78	22.22
22	5.55	4.44	19	28.33	22.67
21	6.11	4.89	20	28.89	23.11
20	6.67	5.33	21	29.44	23.56
19	7.22	5.78	22	30	24
18	7.78	6.22	23	30.55	24.44
17	8.33	6.67	24	31.11	24.89
16	8.89	7.12	25	31.67	25.33
15	9.44	7.56	26	32.22	25.78
14	10	8	27	32.78	26.22
13	10.55	8.44	28	33.33	26.67
12	11.11	8.89	29	33.89	27.11
11	11.67	9.33	30	34.44	27.56
10	12.22	9.78	31	35	28
9	12.78	10.22	32	35.55	28.44
8	13.33	10.67	33	36.11	28.89
7	13.89	11.11	34	36.67	29.33
6	14.44	11.56	35	37.22	29.78
5	15	12	36	37.78	30.22
4	15.55	12.44	37	38.33	30.67
3	16.11	12.89	38	38.89	31.11
2	16.67	13.33	39	39.44	31.56
1	17.22	13.78	40	40	32
0	17.78	14.22			

VIII. *Comparison between the Scale of Celsius and those of Réaumur and Fahrenheit.*

Celsius.	Réaumur.	Fahrenheit.	Celsius.	Réaumur.	Fahrenheit.
+100	+80	+212	+61	+48.8	+141.8
99	79.2	210.2	60	48	140
98	78.4	208.4	59	47.2	138.2
97	77.6	206.6	58	46.4	136.4
96	76.8	204.8	57	45.6	134.6
95	76.	203	56	44.8	132.8
94	75.2	201.2	55	44	131
93	74.4	199.4	54	43.2	129.2
92	73.6	197.6	53	42.4	127.4
91	72.8	195.8	52	41.6	125.6
90	72	194	51	40.8	123.8
89	71.2	192.2	50	40	122
88	70.4	190.4	49	39.2	120.2
87	69.6	188.6	48	38.4	118.4
86	68.8	186.8	47	37.6	116.6
85	68	185	46	36.8	114.8
84	67.2	183.2	45	36	113
83	66.4	181.4	44	35.2	111.2
82	65.6	179.6	43	34.4	109.4
81	64.8	177.8	42	33.6	107.6
80	64	176	41	32.8	105.8
79	63.2	174.2	40	32	104
78	62.4	172.4	39	31.2	102.2
77	61.6	170.6	38	30.4	100.4
76	60.8	168.8	37	29.6	98.6
75	60	167	36	28.8	96.8
74	59.2	165.2	35	28	95
73	58.4	163.4	34	27.2	93.2
72	57.6	161.6	33	26.4	91.4
71	56.8	159.8	32	25.6	89.6
70	56	158	31	24.8	87.8
69	55.2	156.2	30	24	86
68	54.4	154.4	29	23.2	84.2
67	53.6	152.6	28	22.4	82.4
66	52.8	150.8	27	21.6	80.6
65	52	149	26	20.8	78.8
64	51.2	147.2	25	20	77
63	50.4	145.4	24	19.2	75.2
62	49.6	143.6	23	18.4	73.4

TABLE VIII.—*Continued.*

Celsius.	Réaumur.	Fahrenheit.	Celsius.	Réaumur.	Fahrenheit.
+22	+17.6	+71.6	—10	—8	+14
21	16.8	69.8	11	8.8	12.2
20	16	68	12	9.6	10.4
19	15.2	66.2	13	10.4	8.6
18	14.4	64.4	14	11.2	6.8
17	13.6	62.6	15	12	5
16	12.8	60.8	16	12.8	3.2
15	12	59	17	13.6	1.4
14	11.2	57.2	18	14.4	— 0.4
13	10.4	55.4	19	15.2	2.2
12	9.6	53.6	20	16	4
11	8.8	51.8	21	16.8	5.8
10	8	50	22	17.6	7.6
9	7.2	48.2	23	18.4	9.4
8	6.4	46.4	24	19.2	11.2
7	5.6	44.6	25	20	13
6	4.8	42.8	26	20.8	14.8
5	4	41	27	21.6	16.6
4	3.2	39.2	28	22.4	18.4
3	2.4	37.4	29	23.2	20.2
2	1.6	35.6	30	24	22
1	0.8	33.8	31	24.8	23.8
0	0	32	32	25.6	25.6
—1	—0.8	30.2	33	26.4	27.4
2	1.6	28.4	34	27.2	29.2
3	2.4	26.6	35	28	31
4	3.2	24.8	36	28.8	32.8
5	4	23	37	29.6	34.6
6	4.8	21.2	38	30.4	36.4
7	5.6	19.4	39	31.2	38 2
8	6.4	17.6	40	32	40
9	7.2	15.8			

IX. *Comparison between the Scale of Réaumur and those of Fahrenheit and Celsius.*

Réaumur.	Fahrenheit.	Celsius.	Réaumur.	Fahrenheit.	Celsius.
+80	+212	+100	+42	+126.50	+52.50
79	209.75	98.75	41	124.25	51.25
78	207.50	97.50	40	122	50
77	205.25	96.25	39	119.75	48.75
76	203	95	38	117.50	47.50
75	200.75	93.75	37	115.25	46.25
74	198.50	92.50	36	113	45
73	196.25	91.25	35	110.75	43.75
72	194	90	34	108.50	42.50
71	191.75	88.75	33	106.25	41.25
70	189.50	87.50	32	104	40
69	187.25	86.25	31	101.75	38.75
68	185	85	30	99.50	37.50
67	182.75	83.75	29	97.25	36.25
66	180.50	82.50	28	95	35
65	178.25	81.25	27	92.75	33.75
64	176	80	26	90.50	32.50
63	173.75	78.75	25	88.25	31.25
62	171.50	77.50	24	86	30
61	169.25	76.25	23	83.75	28.75
60	167	75	22	81.50	27.50
59	164.75	73.75	21	79.25	26.25
58	162.50	72.50	20	77	25
57	160.25	71.25	19	74.75	23.75
56	158	70	18	72.50	22.50
55	155.75	68.75	17	70.25	21.25
54	153.50	67.50	16	68	20
53	151.25	66.25	15	65.75	18.75
52	149	65	14	63.50	17.50
51	146.75	63.75	13	61.25	16.25
50	144.50	62.50	12	59	15
49	142.25	61.25	11	56.75	13.75
48	140	60	10	54.50	12.50
47	137.75	58.75	9	52.25	11.25
46	135.50	57.50	8	50	10
45	133.25	56.25	7	47.75	8.75
44	131	55	6	45.50	7.50
43	128.75	53.75	5	43.25	6.25

TABLE IX.—*Continued.*

Réaumur.	Fahrenheit.	Celsius.	Réaumur.	Fahrenheit.	Celsius.
+4	+41	+5	—15	— 1.75	—18.75
3	38.75	3.75	16	4	20
2	36.50	2.50	17	6.25	21.25
1	34.25	1.25	18	8.50	22.50
0	32	0	19	10.75	23.75
—1	29.75	—1.25	20	13	25
2	27.50	2.50	21	15.25	26.25
3	25.25	3.75	22	17.50	27.50
4	23	5	23	19.75	28.75
5	20.75	6.25	24	22	30
6	18.50	7.50	25	24.25	31.25
7	16.25	8.75	26	26.50	32.50
8	14	10	27	28.75	33.75
9	11.75	11.25	28	31	35
10	9.50	12.50	29	33.25	36.25
11	7.25	13.75	30	35.50	37.50
12	5	15	31	37.75	38.75
13	2.75	16.25	32	40	40
14	0.50	17.50			

II.

MEASURES OF WEIGHT.

TABLE X.

AVOIRDUPOIS WEIGHT.

Drachms.	Ounces.	Pounds.	Quarters.	Cwt.	Ton.
16	1				
256	16	1			
7,168	448	28	1		
28,672	1,792	112	4	1	
573,440	35,840	2,240	80	20	1

The standard avoirdupois pound of the United States, as determined by Mr. Hassler, is the weight of 27.7015 cubic inches of distilled water (1 gallon contains 231 cubic inches), weighed in air, at the temperature of the maximum density (39.83° Fahr.), the barometer being at 30 inches.

TABLE XI.

Troy Weight.

Grains.	Dwt.	Ounce.	Pound.
24	1		
480	20	1	
5760	240	12	1

The pound, ounce, and grain are the same in apothecaries' and Troy weight; in the former, the ounce is divided into 8 drachms, the drachm into 3 scruples, and the scruple into 20 grains.

7000	Troy grains =	1 lb.	avoirdupois.
175	Troy pounds =	144 lbs.	"
175	Troy ounces =	192 oz.	"
437½	Troy grains =	1 oz.	"

TABLE XII.

Table of Weights.

Milligramme	=	0.0154	grains Troy.	
Centigramme	=	0.1544	"	
Décigramme	=	1.5444	"	
Gramme	=	15.4440	"	= 0.035 oz. avoirdupois.
Décagramme	=	154.4402	"	
Hectogramme	=	1544.4023	"	
Kilogramme	=	15444.0234	"	= 2.205 lbs. avoirdupois.
Myriogramme	=	154440.2344	"	

The basis of the French system of weights is the weight in vacuo of a litre, or a cubic décimètre, which is equal to 1.0567 quarts, liquid measure, of distilled water at the temperature of 39.2° Fahr. $\frac{1}{1000}$ part of this weight is a gramme.

1 lb. avoirdupois = 0.4535685 kilogramme.
1 litre of distilled water weighs 35.274 ounces avoirdupois.

INDEX.

L.

M.

N.

O.

P.

www.ingramcontent.com/pod-product-compliance
Lightning Source LLC
LaVergne TN
LVHW011220110826
845150LV00006B/1486

* 9 7 8 1 4 2 5 5 1 6 4 6 8 *